# The Magic of Machine Embroidery

Craftworld Books

# Contents

HEARTS & FLOWERS.................................. 4

BLACK SWANS........................................ 10

THE HAPPY HEART CUSHION.................... 16

MACHINE EMBROIDERY FROM THE PAST..... 23

ORIENT EXPRESS.....................................24

LITTLE BLUE WREN.................................30

MACHINE EMBROIDERY TIPS.....................37

COUNTRY COTTAGE CUSHION....................38

ENCHANTED GHOST GUMS........................44

TERRIFIC TIE BACKS...............................50

RURAL ROAD.............................................54

OUT OF THE SHADOWS.............................60

BARGELLO & SEMINOLE QUILTED JACKET....64

TECHNIQUE TUTOR..................................71

TIME FOR TEA........................................72

TRELLIS TREASURE..................................77

BABY, LOOK AT YOU.................................82

HATS OFF TO SUMMER.............................88

GLOSSARY..............................................94

INDEX..................................................95

# Hearts & Flowers

*Like so many modern embellishment methods, the inspiration for machine ribbon embroidery has its origins in the classic techniques of handwork.*
*In this project, by Husqvarna's Larraine Jenkins, you'll learn how to create beautiful silk-ribbon roses and leaves on an exquisite cushion using even the most basic of sewing machines.*

## MATERIALS

- 1 m x 115cm (1¹/₈yd x 45in) silk dupion
- 60cm x 115cm (⁵/₈yd x 45in) silk dupion for centre contrast (heart)
- Machine embroidery thread, colour to tone with the main fabric
- Silk ribbons 4mm (¹/₈in) and 7mm (¹/₄in) widths:
  For each rose allow 40cm (16in) — large roses are made from 7mm (¹/₄in) ribbon, small roses from 4mm (¹/₈in).
  Allow 15cm (6in) of 4mm (¹/₈in) silk ribbon for each leaf cluster.
- One reel of monofilament thread
- One reel of Bobbinfil, white
- Machine needle, universal 80/12
- 1 m x 45cm (1¹/₈yd x 18in) fusible interfacing
- 25cm (10in) square of Vliesofix (paper-backed fusible web)
- One 30cm (12in) zipper
- Non-permanent fabric marker
- Overlocker tweezers or a bamboo satay stick
- Embroidery scissors
- 12cm (4³/₄in) spring embroidery hoop
- Machine feet: braiding, candlewicking and ruffler or gathering
- Machine quilting guide
- 35cm (13³/₄in) cushion insert

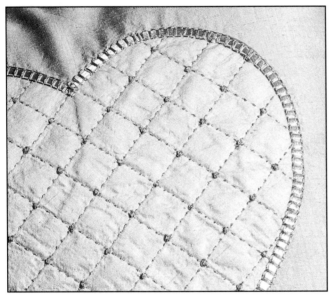

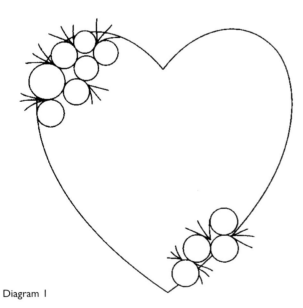

Diagram 1

## METHOD

1. Cut two 38cm (15in) squares from the main fabric for the front and back of the cushion. Cut one 25cm (10in) square of contrast fabric for the heart appliqué.

2. Fuse the interfacing to the wrong side of the three fabric pieces to add support and body.

3. Fuse the square of Vliesofix to the back of the contrast fabric. Trace the heart pattern from the pattern sheet onto the paper side of the Vliesofix and cut out the heart shape. Remove the paper backing and fuse the heart shape in position on the centre front of the cushion.

4. Mark a diagonal line across the heart with the fabric marker. Place the monofilament thread on top of the machine, and embroidery thread in the bobbin. Sew along the diagonal line using a mock hand-quilting stitch. Refer to your machine's instruction manual for tension adjustments if necessary.

> ## TIPS • If your machine doesn't have a specialised mock hand-quilting stitch, use a triple straight stitch.
> • All marking pens should be pre-tested on a scrap of fabric to ensure the marks will be easily removed.

5. Sew parallel rows at 2cm ($^3/_4$in) intervals using the machine quilting guide for accuracy. When the diagonal lines have been completed, mark a line at right angles and repeat with parallel rows of stitching as before to form a diamond pattern on the heart.

6. Place the embroidery thread through the top of the machine and attach the candlewicking foot. Refer to your machine's instructions on programming a single candlewicking stitch and place one stitch at each diamond junction to replace the traditional hand-stitched knot.

> ## TIP If your machine can't sew a candlewicking stitch, hand-sew a knot at each diamond junction.

7. Attach the braiding foot to the machine and select the heirloom ladder stitch. Position the 4mm ($^1/_8$in) ribbon under the presser foot and stitch around the raw edge of the heart shape, forming a decorative border. Begin sewing the border design where the large roses will be positioned.

8. Trace the heart design from the pattern sheet onto paper and draw the placement for the roses and the leaves before marking the fabric. To gauge the size of the roses, draw them

as circles and the leaves as lines. When the placement is satisfactory, transfer the design to the cushion front with the non-permanent marker. See diagram 1.

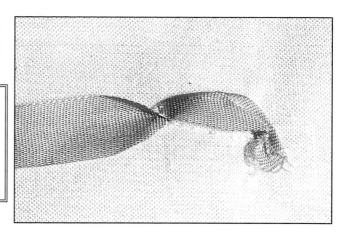

> # TIPS
> • Three strands of ribbon floss threaded through the centre grooves of a seven groove cording foot will give an interesting variation on the heirloom ladder stitch.
> • If your machine can't sew an heirloom ladder stitch, use a simple, utility blanket stitch.

9. Place a sample piece of fabric in the embroidery hoop to test the silk ribbon technique.

**Machine Set-up:**

| | |
|---|---|
| Machine foot | Foot removed |
| Needle | 80 |
| Top thread | Monofilament |
| Bobbin thread | Bobbinfil |
| Feed teeth | Lowered |
| Stitch length | 0 |
| Stitch width | 0 |

Set the machine for needle stop down if possible.

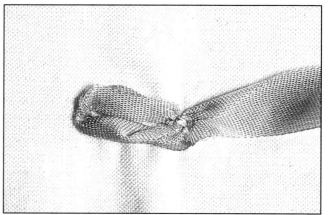

10. Place the hoop with the sample fabric on the machine. Sew a few stitches in the fabric without moving the hoop to secure the thread ends.

> # TIP
> To create a beautiful shadow effect in leaves and flowers, use variegated silk ribbons.

## LEAVES

1. Begin to stitch the leaves by placing one end of ribbon under the needle and securing it in place with a few stitches.

2. Move the hoop away from the needle and walk the needle to the end of the leaf. Leave the needle in the fabric. Hold the ribbon across the front of the needle with a pair of overlocker tweezers or a short satay stick to anchor it in place.

3. Pivot the work and walk the needle back to the start of the leaf, leaving the needle down in the fabric. Hold the ribbon across the needle and anchor it in place.

4. Repeat this method for two more leaves to form a cluster. To finish, cut the ribbon with embroidery scissors leaving a 6mm ($^1/_4$in) tail. Tuck the tail under the last leaf and anchor it.

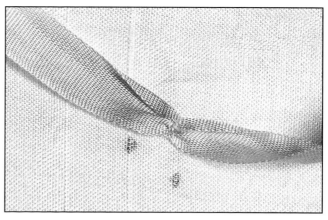

## ROSES

1. Each rose requires 40cm (16in) of ribbon. Use 7mm ($^1/_4$in) ribbon for the large roses and 4mm ($^1/_8$in) ribbon for the small roses. Cut the ribbon to length.

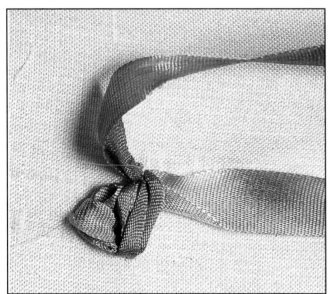

2. Mark three dots 6mm ($^1$/$_4$in) apart in a triangle pattern. Fold the ribbon in half and stitch the centre to one of the dots.

3. Walk the needle to the next dot, leave the needle in the fabric when you get there. Cross the ribbon in front of the needle. Stitch the ribbon in place.

4. Hold the ribbon ends away from the needle and walk to the next dot. Leave the needle in the fabric and cross over both ends of the ribbon in front of the needle. Stitch the ribbon in place. This forms the centre of the rose.

5. Continue to stitch the ribbon in an outwards radiating spiral pattern. Increase the petal lengths, anchoring ribbon twists at each point, until the rose reaches the desired diameter. See diagram 2.

6. Leave a 6mm ($^1$/$_4$in) tail on each ribbon, then cut the ends. Tuck the ends under the last petal and anchor them in place.

7. Stitch all of the roses in the appropriate position, adjusting the sizes to suit the design.

## FINISHING

Cut three strips across the width of the fabric for each frill. Cut strips 18cm (7in) wide for the outer frill and 12cm (4$^3$/$_4$in) wide for the narrow frill. Join the seams to form a circle for each frill. Fold the strips lengthwise and baste the raw edges together. Attach the ruffler or the gathering foot and pleat or gather the frill. Baste both frills to the front of the embroidered fabric and complete the cover as you would a standard cushion. ✂

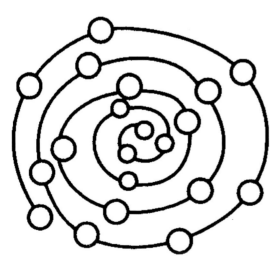

Diagram 2

# Black Swans

Stewart Merrett designed
these regal black swans for
the cocktail bar of the Regent
Hotel in Melbourne. Although
the originals are larger than
lifesize, the pattern can be
made any size you wish for a
cushion or wallhanging.

1. Enlarge the design. This shows the overhead projector method, but you could scale up by hand or use a photocopier.

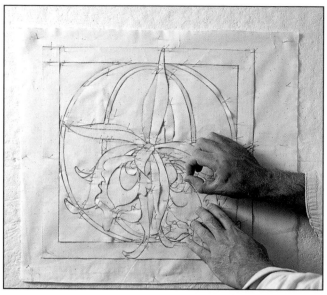

3. Pin one copy of the pattern onto a pin board to be used as a placement pattern. Cut the shapes from the other pattern and pin them in position on the placement pattern.

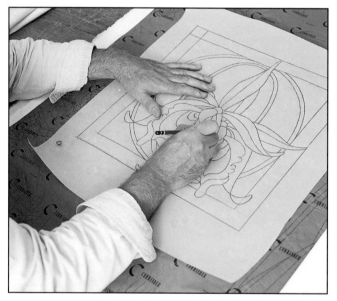

2. Using two sheets of carbon paper and two pieces of calico, trace two copies of the pattern.

4. Remove the shapes from the placement pattern, one colour group at a time and keep in separate piles. Place the calico pieces of one colour group right side up on newspaper and spray with adhesive.

## MATERIALS

- Tracing Paper
- Pencil
- Ruler and set square (if enlarging by hand)
- Carbon paper
- Calico
- Scissors
- Spray adhesive
- Protective mask
- Newspapers

- Selection of fabric scraps
- Fabric for backing the design
- Dacron batting
- Machine threads

NOTE: The step-by-step photographs are a guide to the technique only. They are not actual photographs of this project in progress. Although the subject matter is different, the method is exactly the same.

5. Place the sticky side of the calico on the wrong side of your chosen applique fabric. Press with a warm iron and cut out the shapes.

7. Position the pieces firmly onto the placement pattern, pressing firmly to attach them securely.

6. Place the selected jigsaw pieces face down on newspaper and thoroughly spray the calico backing with adhesive.

8 Continue adding the pieces until all shapes are adhered to the placement pattern and your jigsaw is complete

Initially, this technique may look complicated but by reading the following and studying the step-by-step photographs all will become clear.

> TIP If you choose to work in black velvet, vary the nap direction of the pieces to achieve a light and shadow effect. Do this by placing the cut out shapes at different angles on the velvet.

1. Using your preferred method, enlarge the design to whatever measurement you require.

2. Trace the design onto two pieces of calico.

3. Pin one tracing to a pin board to become the placement pattern.

4. Cut the shapes from the other tracing and then pin them in position on the placement pattern.

5. Choose the fabrics for your appliqué.

6. Then remove the pinned on shapes from the placement

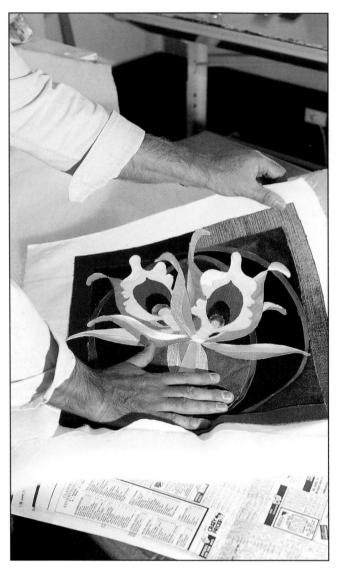

9. Remove the assembled design from the pin board and spray the back with adhesive. Press the sticky side to the Dacron batting and trim the edges.

10. Place the trimmed design face down and spray the Dacron batting with adhesive.

pattern, taking all the pieces to be worked in one colour and keeping them in a group before removing all the pieces of the next colour.

7. Continue working in this way until all the pieces are removed and sorted into piles of their respective colour groups.

> TIP If your fabrics require ironing, iron on the back with a warm iron.

8. Still keeping your calico pieces in their colour groups, place the pieces right side up on a newspaper covered surface in a well ventilated room and spray with adhesive. Remember to wear a face mask when spraying adhesive.

9. Place the sprayed calico pieces sticky side down on the wrong side of the appropriate fabric and press with a warm iron. Continue until you have used up all the calico shapes.

10. Then cut out the calico backed appliqué pieces which will resemble bits of a jigsaw.

11. Sort out the order in which you wish to add the pieces to the placement pattern. Place the selected jigsaw pieces face down on fresh newspaper and thoroughly spray the calico backing with spray adhesive.

12. Firmly press the pieces in position on the placement pattern. Continue working in this way until all pieces are in place.

**13.** Take the fully assembled design from the pin board, and place face down on fresh newspaper to spray adhesive on the calico backing.

**14.** Press the sticky side of the design onto a piece of Dacron batting a little larger than the design. Trim the edges.

**15.** Turn the assembly over and spray the Dacron batting with adhesive.

**16.** Press the sticky Dacron to the backing fabric.

**17.** Satin stitch around each shape, through all the layers. Perspectively speaking, start at the back of your image and work towards the front of the design, sewing over or across all untidy ends.

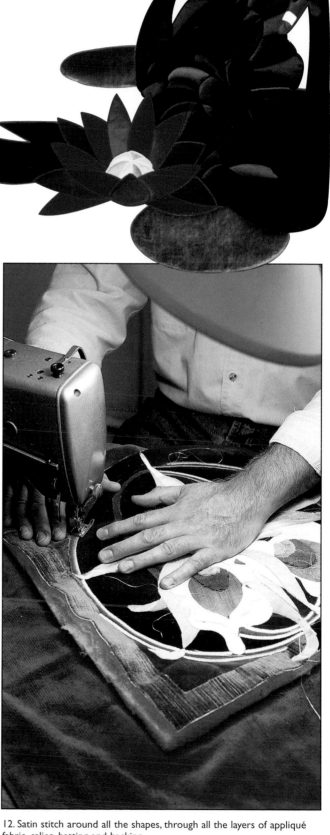

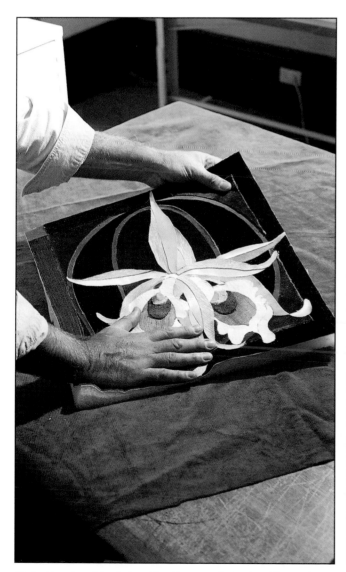

11. Position the sticky design right side up on the backing fabric and press by hand to adhere.

12. Satin stitch around all the shapes, through all the layers of appliqué fabric, calico, batting and backing.

# The Happy Heart Cushion

*Gabriella Verstraeten says this cushion cover is not as complicated as it looks! The majority of sewing is done with a straight stitch, a little zigzag and some decorative stitches. Raw edges, wiggly lines, contrasting bold colours and uneven stitching are all characteristics that add to the freedom and happiness of the design.*

## MATERIALS

- 45cm deep blue satin for the base cloth
- 45cm lightweight Dacron batting
- 45cm Bemsilk lining
- 75cm Vliesofix (paper backed fusible webbing)
- 10cm red satin
- 10cm mustard satin
- 10cm orange satin
- 45cm patterned or coloured fabric for cushion back
- 1.70m flanged piping cord (optional)
- Sewing threads: one in white, two in colour of base cloth
- Machine embroidery threads: two reels each of red, deep yellow, turquoise, blue, orange
- Sewing machine needles: 130N Size 90 Schmetz
- One pair twin needles: 1.6/70 or 2.0/80 or 2.5/80
- Scissors for paper, fabric, embroidery
- Appliqué mat
- Dressmaker's square
- Tailors chalk
- Spray starch
- Steam iron
- Old blanket and towed for a make shift ironing board surface to lay your appliqué out on
- Masking tape
- Pins and a hand sewing needle
- Unpicker

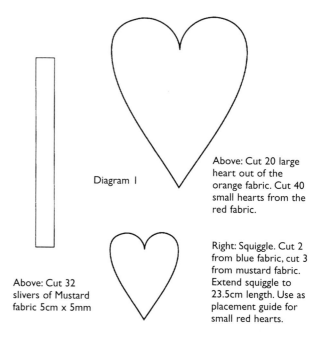

Diagram 1

Above: Cut 32 slivers of Mustard fabric 5cm x 5mm

Above: Cut 20 large heart out of the orange fabric. Cut 40 small hearts from the red fabric.

Right: Squiggle. Cut 2 from blue fabric, cut 3 from mustard fabric. Extend squiggle to 23.5cm length. Use as placement guide for small red hearts.

## PREPARING THE APPLIQUÉ PIECES

From the blue base cloth cut a piece 14cm x 28cm. Fuse strips of Vliesofix to the wrong side of this piece. Do the same with the red and the mustard fabrics. Use your appliqué mat to protect the iron.

Make sure the rough side of the Vliesofix lies down on the wrong side of the coloured fabrics.

From each of these fabrics cut the following shapes.

- **Red fabric:** four strips 1cm x 25cm, 40 small hearts (see diagram 1).
- **Mustard fabric:** two strips 5cm x 25cm three large squiggles, 32 slivers 5cm x 5mm.
- **Blue fabric:** two large squiggles.
- **Orange fabric:** Twenty large hearts (see diagram 1)

To cut out the multi shapes, fold the fabric fused with Vliesofix concertina style. Pin and with paper scissors cut out more than one shape at once. Keep appliqué shapes to one side.

## PREPARING THE BASE CLOTH OF THE CUSHIONS FOR APPLIQUÉ

Cut the base cloth, batting and lining 43cm square. Cut two squares of Vliesofix 41cm square.

Put batting, lining and Vliesofix to one side. Lay out the old blanket and towel for your makeshift ironing board and put the base cloth on top.

Using the dressmaker's square and tailor's chalk mark in the following lines. (See diagram 2). Rule in on all sides from the edges, lines at the following intervals: 1.5cm, 4cm, 9cm.

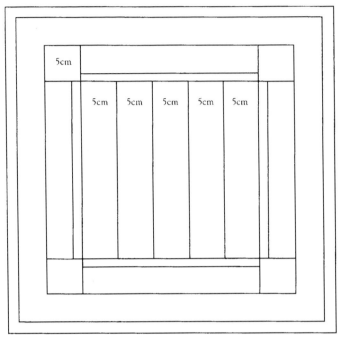

Diagram 2: (Not to scale. All measurements in centimetres.)

The inner square will divide lengthwise into five columns, each 5cm wide. Mark in with tailor's chalk.

Machine or hand tack on all of these lines. Spray starch and press. These lines will become your placement guide lines for your appliqué pieces.

On the second and fourth columns of the inner square, lay down the two mustard coloured strips (5cm x 25cm), after peeling away the paper backing. Fuse these columns into position.

On top of these mustard columns centre the two blue squiggles. Fuse in place. On the alternate blue columns fuse the mustard coloured squiggles down the centre.

Now place and fuse each of the red strips (1cm x 25cm) on the outer edges of the inner square.

The 40 little red hearts are positioned next. Each column in the inner square has eight hearts. The hears are positioned in the negative spaced created by the squiggle. Fuse in place. On the next outer border (directly below the red strip) place six orange hearts either side of the inner square.

In each of the border corners lay a grid of four strips by four strips cut from the left over mustard fabric (see diagram 3).

## PREPARE THE CUSHION TOP FOR SEWING

Turn the cushion top over. Fuse one 41cm square piece of the Vliesofix to the wrong side. Peel away the paper backing. Put to one side. Lay down the Bemsilk lining. Repeat as above. Leave on the ironing surface. Place the dacron batting on top of the silk lining.

Now take the cushion top and place on top to create sandwich. Using an appliqué mat and your iron, fuse al the layers together.

## STITCHING SEQUENCE

1. Using a colour matched mustard embroidery thread, appliqué the outer edges of the mustard coloured columns:
**Appliqué foot**
**Decorative Stich:** W 5, L 0.5
**Upper Tension:** Loose

2. Using a contrast colour upper thread appliqué the squiggles. Select one of the decorative stitches thas has a satin stitch component to it (see photograph 1):
**Appliqué foot**
**Decorative Stitch:** W 5, L 0.5
**Upper Tension:** Loose

3. **Red inner border strips:** Using a colour matched upper thread appliqué using the same setting as in step 1. At the same time do the row of zigzag stitching to make the red squares in each corner that contain the mustard coloured grids.

Diagram 3: (Not to scale)

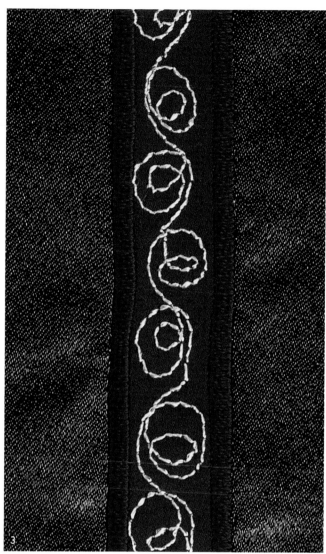

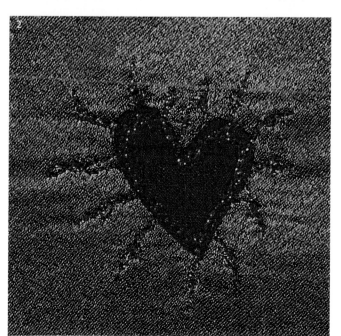

**4. Small red hearts:**
Continue with the red thread. Set machine to do freehand machine embroidery:
**Darning foot**
**Straight stich**
**Stich length:** 0
**Upper Tension:** Loose
**Feed dogs:** lowered

Straight stich around each heart a couple of times. Once secured, add little squiggles that radiate out all around (see photograph 2). Do this by stitching out from the heart, hovering while stitching, then sew back to the heart. Move on to the next heart and repeat the sequence.

**5. Mustard circles:** Change to mustard thread on top. Keep the machine set for freehand machine embroidery. On the red border line, using a straight stich, sew a continuous row of circles (see photograph 3).

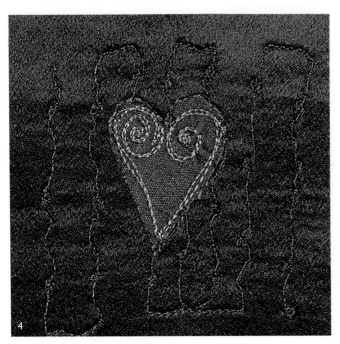

tension disc and at the needle guide loop. Make sure the thread comes off the reels in opposite directions. Put two contrast colours on top. (I have used orange and turquoise) With the machine still set for freehand machine embroidery, straight stich a grid directly on top of the appliqué pieces (see photo 5).

**9. Red outer border:** Reset machine for appliqué, raise feed dogs. Change to red thread, appliqué foot, zigzag stich W4, L 0.5. Remove twin needle, use single needle and one thread. Zigzag on the tacking stich of border line which the orange hearts sit on.

**6. Orange hearts:** Keep the machine and thread as is. Stich each orange heart down with this pattern. See photograph 4.

**7.** Change to orange thread and straight stich behind the orange hearts, creating continuous columns of wobbly lines that have little knobbles as you stich. To create these knobbles you need to hover in one spot and stich circles on top of each other. Tis will create a random stripe which appears to be behind the orange hearts.

**8. Mustard grid:** Using twin needles, thread the machine just as you would for a single needle, but split the threads at the

10. **Outer border:** Set machine for freehand machine embroidery as in point 4 and straight stich, thread with turquoise on top. In the very outer border stich blocks of rows of straight stich all in one direction, about 2cm apart. Stich all around the outer edge. Rethread with orange. Repeat the stitching sequence as above, but at right angles to the previous stitching (see photograph 6).

11. **Outer red border.** Repeat as for step 9, but on the line marked at 1.5cm in from the cut edge.

12. Remove any visible tacking stiches. Press, trim and overlock the outer edges.

13. See instructions for finishing the cushion. The following are guidelines only. Sewers should consult their handbooks for any specific modifications required for their own machine.

## SETTING UP THE MACHINE FOR FREE-MOTION SEWING

| | |
|---|---|
| **Foot:** | Darning |
| **Feed dog:** | Lowered |
| **Stitch:** | Straight |
| **Stitch length:** | 0 |
| **Upper tension:** | Loosen |
| **Machine needle:** | 130N size 90 |

**Machine technique:** Move the foot pedal down flat out, as fast as you can go.

**Fabric movement:** Move the fabric in a steady, smooth movement as if you were panning for gold.

**Beginning:** Make sure you bring the lower thread up through the needle before you begin to sew. Hold on to both the top and bottom threads as you begin to stitch.

**Securing threads:** A few stiches up and down in one spot will secure the threads.

## SEWING NOTIONS

• Bobbin thread is a normal sewing thread throughout the project. The colour of the thread is matched to the base colour of the cushion cover.

• Any decorative stitching is done with machine embroidery thread on top and normal sewing thread in the bobbin.

• Any making up and regular sewing uses normal sewing thread.

• The same needle type and size has been used throughout the project.

## MAKING UP THE CUSHION COVERS

### Cushion backs

Cut two pieces 45 x 32cm. On one long edge of each piece fold and press over 1cm and then another 2cm. Straight stitch down and place pieces to one side.

### Piping

• Trim and square the cushion top. Overlock the raw edge.

• Unpick the first 5cm of one edge of the piping cord and tape. Place the masking tape over the threads to stop them fraying. Unpick the tape from the cord and untwist the cords.

• On the unravelled end fold the wrapped cords over at a 90 degrees angle to the cotton tape ensuring they keep the colour sequence they were twisted in. Straight stich them down across the front of the tape to hold them in place (not the red stitching).

• Pin the flanged cord around the outer edge of the cushion top. The cord lies on the inside and the edge of the tape lines up with the outer edge.

• At the corners, clip the flanged tape to within 5mm of the stitching at the three places on the corner. Now manipulate the cord to turn making a rounded square finish.

• Pin until you arrive at the joining point. Unpick and unravel the other end of the flanged cord back to that point. Place masking tape on the ends of the tape and cord to prevent unravelling.

• Fold the cords down to the front of the tape in their twisting sequence. Stitch to secure. (Red stitching.)

• Lay the end of the cord over the starting end of the cord. They should match up, hiding the join.

• Hand tack in place.

• Machine stitch in place as close to the cord as possible using the zipper foot, straight stitch at L3, normal upper tension and a far left needle position.

• Now lay one of the backs of the cushion cover pieces you prepared earlier on top of the embroidered cushion top, right sides together. The turned edge goes across the cushion back. Pin across the top edge as close as possible to the piping.

• Repeat with the other backing piece on the opposite edge.

• Pin on all sides.

• Machine stitch the backing and cushion top together using the same machine setting as for the piping cord.

• Clip the corners. Turn inside out and press. ✄

Attaching cord to a cushion top.

# Machine Embroidery from the Past

Compiled with assistance from Marie Cavanagh Custodian of the collection of the Embroiderers Guild of NSW.

*"Our hope is that no longer will the family sewing machine be regarded merely as the household drudge for sewing long seams, but as a means for enjoyment in producing beautiful decorative needlework."*

These words were written by Dorothy Benson in the foreword of her book, Machine Embroidery – The Artistic Possibilities of the Domestic Sewing Machine, published circa 1920.

The domestic sewing machine referred to was a Singer straight stitch treadle machine and considerable skill was required to produce examples like the one shown. Mrs Rachel Aisenberg may have referred to this book when she embroidered her sampler.

Examples of thread painting – filling in areas with smooth zigzag stitches – satin stitch, corded satin stitch, whip stitch, cutwork, drawn threadwork and lacework were painstakingly embroidered on natural coloured linen.

To achieve an even zigzag stitch, the fabric was tightly stretched in an embroidery hoop. The hoop was moved from side to side by hands moving in perfect harmony with the rhythm of the needle which was kept at a steady speed by even treadling. No easy feat!

From 1919 until 1938 Mrs Aisenberg made her home in Manjollie, a small town near Harbin in Manchuria. The local railway station was featured in the film The Last Emperor. When Mrs Aisenberg moved to Sydney, in the year 1938, her much loved sewing machine accompanied her, and she continued to use it in Australia for many more years, producing beautiful examples like the one shown. ✂

**Below left.** Motif from the embroidered sampler made by Mrs Rachel Aisenberg on a straight stitch Singer treadle machine. Size approximately 6cm x 8cm (2$^1$/$_3$in x 3$^1$/$_3$in). From the Collection of The Embroiderers' Guild of NSW.
**Below right.** Free-machine scribble fills in shapes outlined in heavier stitching.
**Bottom.** Mrs Aisenberg's historic sampler shows experiments with satin stitch, corded couching, whip stitch, drawn threadwork and lacework.

*This elegant, Orient-inspired jacket combines appliqué, quilting and machine-embroidery techniques. MARGARET LAWTIE, creative consultant from the Perth Sewing Centre, made the jacket on Pfaff's 7570 sewing machine and used the Pfaff Creative Fantasy embroidery unit to create the garment's stunning embellishments. Readers without this machine can create their own striking decoration by substituting the Pfaff images with designs from their machine's library, or they may use purchased motifs.*

## MATERIALS

- Any jacket pattern
- Silk dupion for jacket, black
- lm silk dupion, red
- 2.5m(2¹/₂yd) lining
- 2.5m (2¹/₂yd) ironon Pellon
- 3.5m (3¹/₂yd) insertion piping or braid, gold
- 1m Vliesofix paperbacked fusible web
- Two reels of metallic machine embroidery thread, gold
- Two reels of rayon 40 machine embroidery thread, red
- Two reels rayon 40 machine embroidery thread, black
- Bobbinfil thread, black
- Polyester thread, black
- Machine needle: Metalfil 90
- Machine feet: open-toe embroidery, freehand embroidery, zigzag
- Pfaff embroidery card: Fantasy 15
- Machine embroidery hoop
- Tear-away fabric stabiliser
- Chalk pencil
- Long dressmakers ruler

## JACKET EMBROIDERY PLACEMENT

**Method**

1. Fuse the iron on to the wrong side of the black fabric, then cut out pattern pieces.

2. Cut a 30cm (12in) square of Vliesofix. Draw two concentric circles of 15cm (6in) and 25cm (l0in) on the paper backing and fuse to the wrong side of the 30cm (12in) square of contrast red silk fabric.

> **TIP** When tracing onto Vliesofix, mark fabric grain lines so appliqué fabric will match garment fabric.

3. Cut out the outer and inner circles to form a ring of red silk. Use a chalk pencil lightly to divide the circle into quarters.

4. To position the circle for embroidery mark a dotted line down the centre back of the jacket pattern piece. On this line mark a line beginning 14cm (5¹/₂in) from the neck edge and ending 39cm (15¹/₂in) from neck edge. Mark the halfway point in this line and mark and rule a line at right angles 12.5cm (5in) on both sides of the central line.

5. Carefully peel the paper backing from the Vliesofix and position the red silk circle on the jacket back, matching placement lines to the quarter markings.

# Orient Express

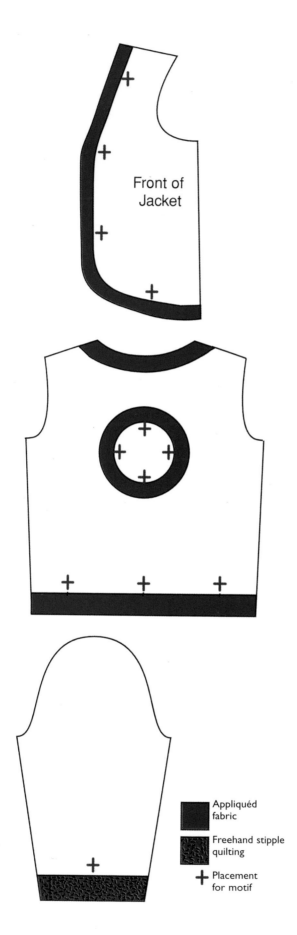

Appliquéd fabric

Freehand stipple quilting

+ Placement for motif

**6.** To form the contrast borders of the jacket, trace the front outer edges of the jacket onto the paper backing of the Vliesofix. Measure and trace a second line 6.5cm (2$\frac{1}{2}$in) inside the first line, following the contours of the edge. Make a mirror-image tracing for the other front piece. Trace a similar 6.5cm (2$\frac{1}{2}$in) border at the neck and hem edge of the jacket back and for the bottom of the sleeves. Mark the jacket pattern pieces in the same way to act as placement lines.

**7.** Roughly cut out the Vliesofix, allowing an extra 2.5cm (1in) outside tracing lines these will be trimmed back later. Fuse the web to the back of red silk fabric, matching grainlines. Trim the fabric to the traced lines.

**8.** Peel the paper from the back of red borders and carefully fuse in place, on right side of jacket pattern pieces, matching placement lines.

**9.** Prepare the machine for appliqué work.
**Machine Set-up:**

| | |
|---|---|
| Machine foot | Satin stitch or open-toe embroidery |
| Needle | Metalfil 90 |
| Top thread | Rayon embroidery, red |
| Bobbin thread | Bobbinfil, black |
| Top tension | Loosened |
| Bobbin tension | Normal |
| Feed teeth | Raised |
| Fabric | Stabilised |

**On a Pfaff machine:**

| | |
|---|---|
| Stitch pattern | Program stitch 60 |
| Stitch length | 10 |
| Stitch width | 5.0 |
| Density | 0.25 |

**On other brands of machine:**
Select a suitable appliqué stitch to cover the raw edges of the appliqué fabrics or use a satin stitch, width 5.0, Length 0.5. Stitch around the outer and inner edges of the circle on the jacket back, the lower edges of the neck band and the upper edge of the bottom of the jacket back and sleeves. On the jacket fronts, stitch the inner edges of the front bands.

**10.** On the inside of the red circle, mark four motif-placement positions 6.5cm (2$\frac{1}{2}$in) from the outside edge. On the lower back border, place one motif in the centre and one 19cm (7$\frac{1}{2}$in) from each side of centre back line. For the front borders, place each motif 7cm (2$\frac{3}{4}$in) from the outside edge,

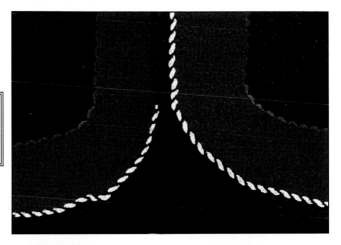

with the top motif 17.5cm (6⁷/₈in) from shoulder seam, then each motif approximately 17.5cm (6⁷/₈in) apart. Place three motifs in this way on each side. The motif on the bottom front is 10.5cm (4in) from the side seam.

> TIP The placement measurements are for size 12 jacket. If you are using a multisize pattern ensure that the motifs are evenly spaced.

11. Embroidering the motifs: Place the embroidery hoop over the area to be embroidered and place tear-away fabric stabiliser underneath.

If applicable, attach the Pfaff Creative Fantasy unit to the machine and select card 15, pattern no 5. Enlarge this to the largest size and embroider using gold thread.

Rotate each motif in the circle so their stems point to the centre. Embroider the motifs on the rest of the garment, arranging them so the stems point towards the centre of the garment.

If you do not have a Pfaff machine, select a suitable motif from your embroidery library and embroider following the placement guidelines.

If your machine cannot embroider, use purchased motifs. When embroidery is complete, remove stabiliser from the back of the work.

12. Remove the embroidery unit and set the machine for freehand embroidery.

**Machine Set-up:**

| | |
|---|---|
| Machine foot | Freehand embroidery |
| Needle | Metalfil 90 |
| Top thread | Rayon embroidery, black |
| Bobbin thread | Bobbinfil, black |
| Top tension | Loosened |
| Bobbin tension | Normal |
| Feed teeth | Lowered or covered |
| Fabric | Stabilised |

Use freehand embroidery to stipple quilt all red areas, moving the fabric in a meandering curving line.

> TIP For an added touch of drama, reverse the jacket's colour scheme to black on red

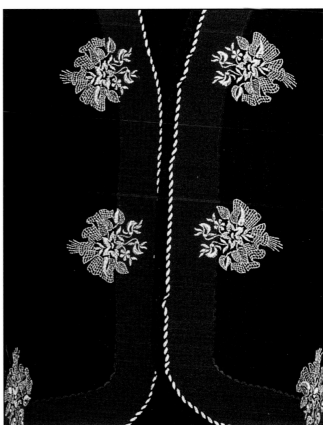

13. Prepare the machine for quilting.

**Machine Set-up:**

| | |
|---|---|
| Machine foot | Zigzag |
| Needle | Metalfil 90 |
| Top thread | Polyester, black |
| Bobbin thread | Polyester, black |
| Top tension | Normal |

| Bobbin tension | Normal |
| --- | --- |
| Feed teeth | Raised |
| Stitch width | 0 |
| Stitch length | 2.5 |

Pin and stitch the jacket side seams, taking care to match bands. Spread the garment flat and using a long dressmakers ruler and a chalk pencil, mark a diagonal line below the circle on the centre back to act as the first quilting guide line.

> TIP A quilting guide attached to the machine foot will make it easy to keep quilting lines evenly spaced.

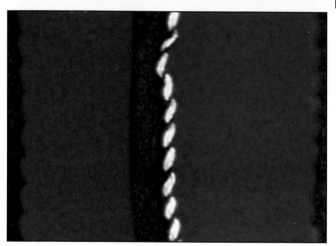

14. Increase the stitch length to 3.0 and stitch a line of quilting. Space quilting lines 5cm (2in) apart. Quilt the back and fronts of the garment, sewing over side seams but avoiding the red circle and the borders. Draw a second guide line beginning on the other side of the jacket, so that subsequent quilting will form diamond patterns. Repeat to quilt sleeves in the same design.

15. Complete jacket and lining according to pattern instructions, attaching insertion piping around entire outside edges of jacket and sleeves. Finish with a bias binding of black fabric. ✂

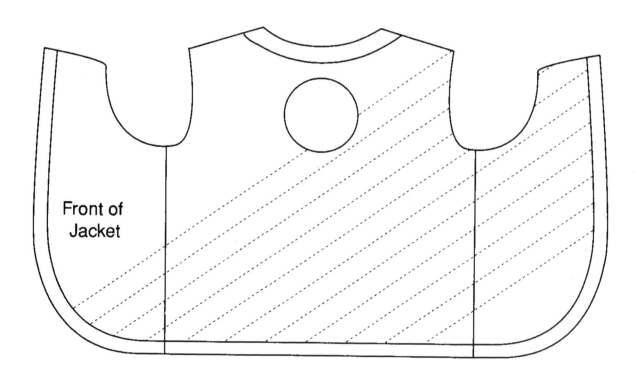

Front of Jacket

# Little Blue Wren

*Inspired by scenes from the Australian bush, textile artist Colleen Price combines freehand machine embroidery and simple fabric printing in this, her creative tribute to our natural heritage.*

## MATERIALS

- Raiman machine embroidery threads, Off white 104, Mid blue 243, Light grey 414, Light blue 239, Dark blue 250, White 101, black 102, Light brown 303, Off white 101, Olive green 419, Mid green 186, Light green 179
- Polyester thread to match background fabric
- Green polyester thread for bobbin
- Madeira Bobbinfil or good quality polyester thread
- 4 x 30cm squares Solvy (cold water soluble fabric)
- 2 x 30cm squares of lightweight interfacing
- Embroidery hoop
- Machine embroidery needle 80/12
- Sewing machine needle Jeans 90/14
- Wooden machine embroidery hoop
- Small sharp embroidery scissors
- Small square of quilt wadding
- Heavyweight iron-on interfacing
- Perma-Set fabric printing inks – light brown, blue, green
- Heavy weight textured fabric at least 10cm larger than finished size of picture
- Rolling pin or bottle
- Paintbrush, pen
- Spoon
- Newspaper, paper towels
- Damp cloth, paper plate
- Small pieces of garden foliage, leaves, ferns, flowers etc
- Picture frame 37cm x 29cm

## PRINTING BACKGROUND FABRIC

1. Cover work surface with newspaper. Place small amount of each coloured ink on paper plate, keeping colours separate. Place a leaf on the newspaper, and use the paintbrush to cover the surface with ink.

2. Lay the leaf, painted side down, in position on the fabric, and use the rolling pin to apply firm pressure, rolling from the bottom to the top of the leaf. Remove the rolling pin as soon as it reaches the top of the leaf, so you don't get excess paint on your fabric. Wipe the rolling pin clean with the damp cloth before printing the next leaf.

   The same leaf can be re-used until it fails to produce a clear image. Six or seven prints should be sufficient for a background, depending on the size of the leaves.

3. After printing, allow the fabric to dry, then press between sheets of newspaper, using the wool setting on the iron, to make the colour permanent. Iron the interfacing to the back of the fabric to create a firm fabric for embroidery.

> **TIP** It's a good idea to practise on a scrap of fabric first, experimenting with different blends of colours. It's not necessary to clean the leaf between prints, as subtle colour blending and tonal changes will add interest to your work. Don't worry if you get a few extra spots of paint on your work, as this too can add more interest to your finished work.

## EMBROIDERY

Set your machine for free embroidery as follows.
- **Machine foot:** Free embroidery or darning foot
- **Feed teeth:** Lowered (or covered)
- **Needle:** Embroidery 80/12
- **Stitch width:** 3 Stitch length: 0
- **Bobbin thread:** Bobbinfil or good quality polyester
- **Top thread:** Raiman embroidery thread
- **Top tension:** Reduce slightly so bobbin thread does not show

## BIRD

1. Using a pen to give clear, sharp lines, trace pattern of wren from pattern sheet – excluding legs – including all lines and arrows, onto interfacing. Place two layers of interfacing into hoop with pattern on top. Make sure the interfacing is as taut as possible or your work will pucker and distort.

2. Using machine stitches, fill in each area of the bird with the colours indicated in the main picture on the pattern sheet. Move the hoop from side to side to fill in with stitches in the direction of the arrows.

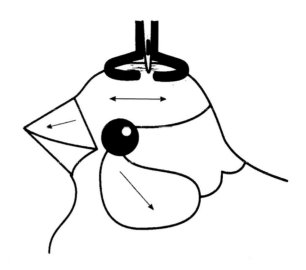

3. Once you have filled in the picture, including the black areas, keep the black thread on the machine and reduce the stitch width to zero. Use this straight stitch to outline and separate each area, feathers around face, wings and tail.

4. Change to white thread. To define the eye area use a stitch width of 1.5 – 2. Keep the embroidery hoop still and sew two small spots in the centre of the eye.

5. Remove work from the hoop and place on top of the wadding. Using a straight stitch and going as close to the embroidery as possible, sew around the outer edges of the bird.

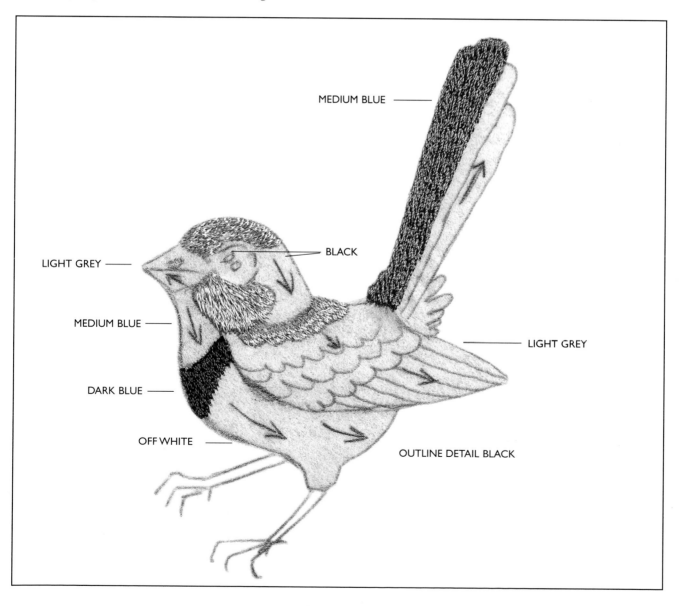

6. Trim excess wadding from the back of the embroidery and cut interfacing 2 – 3mm from the outline stitching. This will allow the bird to be sewn on the background fabric with a very small zigzag stitch.

> TIPS Before starting a project do a small test sample to check machine thread tension. Always lower the machine presser foot before beginning to sew. This will engage the machine's top tension and avoid thread bunching and forming large loops beneath your work.

## BRANCH

1. Prepare and trace pattern as you did for the bird. The branch pattern is on page the pattern sheet.

2. Fill in the branch, using brown thread and following the arrows for the direction of stitching. When the main part of the branch has been embroidered, add several dots to the branch to resemble lichen. To do this thread machine with white thread, select zigzag, set the stitch width to 1.5, and secure the thread.

Sew seven to eight zigzag stitches in the same place, without moving the hoop, allowing the stitches to build up into a small bump of thread. Move the hoop to sew another bump of thread. Move the hoop to sew another bump a few millimetres away. Make a group of about 10 bumps close together.

3. Thread machine with olive green. Set the stitch width to zero and sew lines of straight stitch around and between the bumps.

TO SEW LICHEN

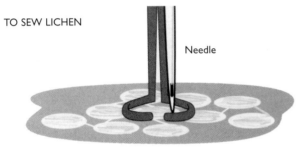

Needle

Sew a zigzag stitch: width is about 1.5 in the same spot allowing the thread to build up.

STITCHING AROUND LICHEN

Close up view of the lichen

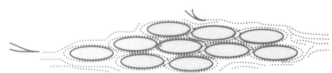

Sew small straight stitches around and in between the white dots on the branch using the olive green thread.

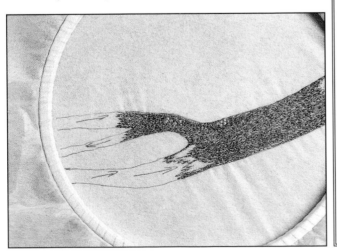

> TIPS • About Solvy: Solvy is a water soluble substance used as a temporary base for stitched thread designs. It acts as a stabiliser until the threads are linked together with enough stitching to support themselves and hold the design firmly. The Solvy is then rinsed away with water leaving only the thread which forms the design. It is important that threads are well linked and attached to the outer edge of the design so it does not fall apart when the Solvy is rinsed away.
> • Keep work tidy and to secure threads, bring the bobbin thread to the top by turning the hand wheel on your machine and pulling on the top thread. Hold the two threads together and do three or four stitches on the spot to secure the threads. Cut the loose threads as close as possible to the stitching. Repeat each time you begin in a new area or with a new thread.

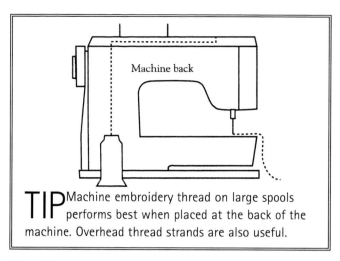

 Machine back

TIP Machine embroidery thread on large spools performs best when placed at the back of the machine. Overhead thread strands are also useful.

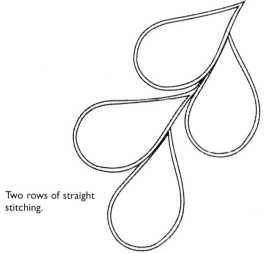

Two rows of straight stitching.

STITCHING LEAVES

## LEAVES

1. Place two layers of Solvy in the hoop and trace the pattern of the leaves from the pattern sheet. Set the machine for freehand machine embroidery as before, with the stitch length and width on zero.

2. The leaves will be seen from both sides, so thread the machine top and bobbin with mid-green polyester thread. Sew around the traced pattern twice with straight stitch, keeping the two rows close together. Return to the centre stem before moving to the next leaf.

3. Change to zigzag stitch, width 3, and fill in each leaf by moving the hoop back and forth. It is important the stitches overlap and link together.

4. When each leaf has been filled with stitching and is well covered, change top thread to the lighter green. Sew around the edge of each leaf with a close zigzag, and sew the veins

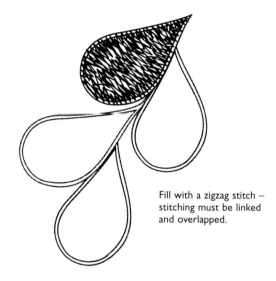

Fill with a zigzag stitch – stitching must be linked and overlapped.

in the same way. You may vary the colours or textures by removing work from the hoop and stitching on the back of the leaves.

5. When the leaves are finished, rinse the work in warm water to remove the Solvy and place flat on a paper towel to dry.

## ASSEMBLING THE PICTURE

1. Pin the branch to the background fabric, and with a small straight stitch, sew down one side close to the edge. Let the thickness of the padding create a gentle bulge and then stitch down the other side.

> **TIP** Don't over-pad the branch, as it will be too hard to attach the bird's body and legs.

2. If necessary, trim the interfacing and blend the edges with small zigzag or straight stitches.

3. Pin the bird into position, allowing for the length of the legs, and attach it in the same way as the branch. Do not distort the bird by holding it too firmly in position as you sew.

4. Thread the needle with black thread and straight stitch around the outside of the bird. Sew the legs and feet with small, close zigzag stitches.

5. Thread the needle with green. Place bunches of leaves in position and secure in several places with small zigzag stitches. Allow the leaves to fall forwards naturally where possible.

6. Secure and trim off any loose threads before framing your work and hanging it with pride. ✄

# Machine Embroidery Tips

Machine embroidery is usually worked over the fabric that is stiffened or stretched to avoid distortion.

Select your stabiliser from the following list:

- **Tear-away stabilisers**

  These add temporary stiffness during embroidery. Perfect for satin-stitched patterns where stabiliser can be easily removed and for art work where permanent stiffness is not a problem. Residue of the tear-away trapped behind stitching will add stiffness to the embroidered area.

- **Chemical stabilisers**

  These types are clear liquids and sprays which lightly stiffen fabric during embroidery. Ideal for long and narrow embroidery areas which cannot be stabilised in a hoop. Suitable for stabilising lightweight washable fabrics, particularly in heirloom sewing Remove by rinsing in cold water.

- **Embroidery hoops**

  Use a hoop to hold fabric firmly for intensive embroidery or finely-detailed areas. Very delicate fabrics such as fine net or tulle should be hooped and further stabilised with a layer of cold water-soluble stabiliser. Hooping is unsuitable for stretch fabrics, or thick-pile fabrics which may be permanently marked by the hoop.

- **Using a hoop**

1. To successfully hoop fabric, make sure the outer and inner hoops fit together snugly. This will be more successful if the inner ring is wrapped with bias tape.
2. Place outer hoop on a table and spread fabric, right side up, over the hoop.
3. Place inner hoop in position and hold the fabric taut with one hand while pressing the hoop into place.
4. Tighten the fabric as much as possible by pulling on excess fabric outside hoop.
5. Release the hoop by pushing up on the inner ring.

- **Securing thread ends**

  Machine-embroider projects involve frequent changes of thread so it is important to learn to secure thread ends.

1. When beginning a new thread, turn the machine's hand wheel so the needle enters the fabric and then returns to its highest point.

2. Pull gently on the needle thread until the bobbin thread comes to the surface of the fabric.
3. Hold the thread ends gently and sew a few small straight stitches. Trim thread ends.
4. Finish each thread by sewing a few small forward and reverse stitches. Trim thread ends.

- **Changing bobbin tension**

  This relates only to machines with a removable bobbin case. As a precaution to losing the small screw in the bobbin case, hold the bobbin case over a small container lined with a tissue.

1. Place a bobbin filled with standard thread in the bobbin case and hold the bobbin case so the open side faces left.
2. Use a small screwdriver to loosen the screw on the side of the case by turning it a few millimetres to the left.
3. Test the tension by suspending the bobbin case by the bobbin thread passed through the spring in the normal way. For the majority of bobbin work, the thread must run freely This means the spring will not support the weight of the bobbin case.
4. If you wish to return the bobbin tension to normal, make a not of how mush the tension was loosened. Remember right is light, left is loose.

- If you plan to do a lot of bobbin work, it may be worth having an extra bobbin case kept specifically for the purpose.

- Consult the machine manual if you own a machine with a drop-in bobbin, as some of these will not take kindly to having their lower tension changed.

- **Changing top tension**

  Most modern machines can be set on automatic or standard tension for ordinary sewing, where the same thread is used in the needle and the bobbin. However, machine embroidery threads require different tensions.

1. The general rule is that the lighter or finer the thread, the looser the tension required. Therefore the tension number will be lower.
2. The wider the stitch, the looser the top tension required, so fine thread will not break and the bobbin thread will not show.

# Country Cottage Cushion

*Capture the ambience of a country cottage garden with this charming painted and machine embroidered cushion by Marilyn Townsend. Clever design creates a framed effect while freehand embroidery leads to flowers and foliage.*

## MATERIALS

- 1m x 1.2m (1¹/₈yd x 47in) of calico
- 30cm (12in) square of polyester wadding
- 30cm (12in) zipper, cream
- Machine feet: satin stitch, freehand embroidery, zigzag, zipper
- Machine needle: embroidery 80
- Several machineembroidery threads in green and floral colours, plus one reel of variegated red
- One reel of polyester thread, cream
- Clear nylon thread for bobbin when working freehand
- Water-erasable marking pen
- Two watercolour paint brushes, sizes 0 and 6
- Plaid brand folk art paints: 424 Light grey, 918 Sunny yellow, 641 Brilliant blue, 412 Magenta, 701 Icy white
- Folkart textile medium
- Saucer or palette for mixing
- Ruler
- One 30cm (12in) cushion insert

## METHOD

1. Cut two pieces of calico 50cm (20in) square. In the centre of one piece, using the watererasable marking pen, trace the design of the cottage and garden. Use the ruler to mark the outlines of the house and roof.

2. Tape the calico to a plastic covered board or table.

3. Mix the paints on the palette or saucer. Read the instructions on the textile medium bottle and use accordingly. If slightly paler colours are required, add a little water. Three shades of green are required, light, mid and dark. To make these, mix three parts yellow to one part blue (light green); equal parts yellow and blue (mid green); and three parts blue to one part yellow (dark green). Experiment on a small piece of calico before painting on the cushion piece and if there is insufficient contrast, add more blue or yellow accordingly. The brown is made by mixing pink, yellow, grey and a little white. Make sure the consistency is not too thin or bleeding will occur. Allow each colour to dry before adding the next. A hair dryer will speed the drying process.

4. Paint all the areas as shown on the design, and when dry, press with a hot, dry iron to fix the colours.

5. Pin the wadding to the underside of the picture.

6. Prepare the sewing machine for embroidery.
**Machine Set-up:**

| | |
|---|---|
| Machine foot | Satin stitch |
| Machine needle | Embroidery 80 |
| Bobbin thread | Clear Nylon |
| Top thread | Machine embroidery, pale grey |
| Top tension | Slightly loosened |
| Bobbin tension | Normal |
| Feed teeth | Raised |
| Stitch pattern | Zigzag |
| Stitch width | 2.0 |
| Stitch length | 0.5 |

7. Work satin stitch along the roof line of the cottage using grey. Outline the doorway in the same way. Change to straight stitch, length 3.0, width 0, and outline the chimney as well as the corner of the house.

8. Prepare the machine for freehand embroidery.
**Machine Set-up:**

| | |
|---|---|
| Machine foot | Freehand embroidery |
| Machine needle | Embroidery 90 |
| Bobbin thread | Clear nylon |

| | |
|---|---|
| Top thread | Machine embroidery, pale grey |
| Top tension | Slightly loosened |
| Bobbin tension | Normal |
| Feed teeth | Lowered or covered |
| Stitch pattern | Zigzag |
| Stitch width | 0 |
| Stitch length | 0 |

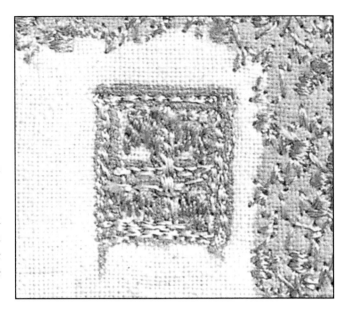

9. Work around the window frames in straight stitch. Then change the top thread to blue and fill in the window panes.

10. Change top thread to brown and straight stitch the trunk and the branches of the right hand tree, stopping with several stitches on the spot to secure the thread as you come to the frame section. Begin again on the other side of the frame, securing the threads at start and finish.

11. Work the left-hand tree using mid green with a stitch varying from straight to wide zigzag, to give the appearance of a wide gum leaf. Practise on a piece of calico first.

All the area of green paint need not be covered as it looks more natural to leave small patches to show through the stitching.

12. Using the same colour through the needle, work the righthand midgreen bush in random zigzag stitch, width 2.0.

13. Change the top thread to light green and stitch the righthand tree in random zigzag stitch, width 1.0, working across the trunk and branches at various places.

14. Continue in the same colour and stitch to work the creeper over part of the roof line.

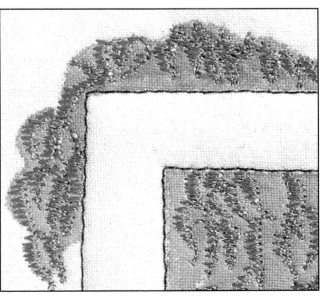

15. Turn the work sideways, increase the stitch width to 3.0, and work across the light-green bush at the left side of the house, leaving an unstitched area under the left window where the hollyhocks will be. Continue working between the gateposts and the fence.

16. Change top thread to midgreen and work the hollyhock leaves in freehand Straight Stitch, moving around in circles.

17. The two areas of dark green in the foreground are worked in straight stitch while moving the work up and down to produce an uneven zigzag. Change to light green and repeat the stitching over the top.

18. Change the top thread to light green to work the two rose bushes in zigzag stitch, width 2.0.

19. Reduce the stitch width to 1.0 and work the creeper over part of the roof edge.

20. Change the top thread to brown and reduce stitch width to 0. Work the fence, gate and the trunks of the two rose bushes.

21. The bright hollyhocks are stitched with a variegated red thread worked around in circles. The deeper red is used at the base and paler pink towards the top.

TIPS Variegated threads are available in an extensive range of colour choices, from subtle light to dark shades of one colour, to bold combinations of primary colours. Before sewing with a variegated thread, make a few stitch samples to determine the arrangement of the colours and how they will look when stitched out.
Care for your cushion by hand-washing in a mild detergent. Rinse well.

22. Embroider the pale pink climber over the edge of the roof, using zigzag stitch worked in small blocks.

23. Depict the mid-green bush on the right-hand side of the picture by using zigzag stitch in wider blocks.

24. Change to white embroidery thread to sew in the roses. Do this with the machine set on zigzag stitch, width 2.0, and work the roses in circles.

25. The lavender in the dark green area on the left-hand side of the foreground, is worked in straight stitch using purple and lilac.

26. When all the embroidery is complete, hold the picture up to ensure there is an even balance of colours. When you are satisfied, prepare machine for straight stitching.

**Machine Set-up:**

| | |
|---|---|
| Machine foot | Zigzag |
| Machine needle | Embroidery 80 |
| Bobbin thread | Clear nylon |
| Top thread | Rayon embroidery, dark green |
| Top tension | Slightly loosened |
| Bobbin tension | Normal |
| Feed teeth | Raised |
| Stitch width | 0 |
| Stitch length | 3.0 |

Stitch along the marked line of the frame, leaving the areas where foliage breaks the line.

27. Trim the wadding close to the embroidery. Around the embroidered cottage, mark a 35cm (14in) square with water-erasable pen. This will be the stitching line for the frill.

28. To make the frill, cut three strips of calico 1.2m x 15cm (47in x 6in). Using the cream polyester sewing thread through the needle and in the bobbin, join the short sides, right sides together, to make a continuous band.

29. Press the seams flat and fold the loop in two, lengthwise, right side out. Press. Overlock or neaten the raw edges and gather to fit around the cushion. Pin and baste the frill around the picture on the sewing line. Stitch on the marked line.

30. Cut the second square of calico in two and insert the zip. With right sides together and the zip open, pin around the frill and trim away the excess fabric.

31. Sew over the existing sewing line. Turn the work right side out and press. Fill with a cushion insert. ✂

# Enchanted Ghost Gums

*The simplicity of heavy calico and the beauty of the Australian bush come together in this jacket by BONNIE BEGG. Inspired by the distinctive leaves and tall trunks of eucalyptus trees and the dangling vines of the rainforest, the jacket makes a subtle yet patriotic statement in wearable art. The jacket was made from a pattern which was Bonnie's own design, but any lined jacket pattern with minimal shaping, no lapels or collar, a slightly extended shoulderline and relaxed sleeveline would be suitable.*

## MATERIALS

- Jacket pattern of your choice
- Heavy-cotton calico fabric enough for jacket plus 50cm
- Two x 1000m reels embroidery thread cols taupe and cream
- 1 x 500m construction thread, col cream
- Machine embroidery needle size 80
- Twin needles 2.5mm and 3mm
- Universal machine needle size 80 for construction
- Crewel hand sewing needle size 9
- Machine feet: zigzag foot, satin stitch and bulky overlock or heavy cording foot
- Water-soluble marking pen
- No More Pins fabric adhesive (optional)
- Fray-stopping liquid
- 20cm Vliesofix
- Crochet thread, col cream
- Selection of gumleaves

Twisted cords and three-dimensional leaves give this garment a hand-crafted look.

**6.** Place the gumleaves onto surplus fabric and trace their outlines with the water-soluble pen. Draw outlines for seven leaves, leaving a 3cm space around each one. Cut out each shape along its 3cm margin.

**7.** Pin one shape in position on the jacket back.
**Machine Set-up:**

| | |
|---|---|
| Machine foot | Zigzag |
| Needle | Size 80 |
| Needle thread | Embroidery, col taupe |
| Bobbin thread | Polyester |
| Feed teeth | Raised |
| Top tension | Normal |
| Bobbin tension | Normal |
| Fabric | Calico |
| Stitch length | 2.0 to 2.5 |
| Stitch width | 0 |

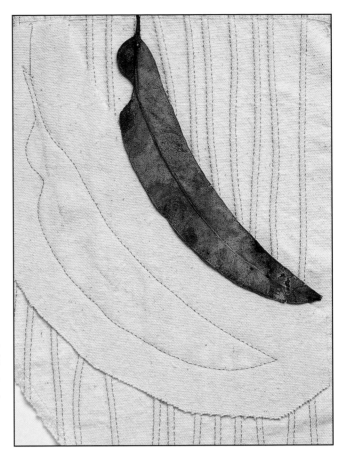

Straight stitch around each leaf shape following the traced line. Using a pair of small, sharp scissors and working close to the stitching line, trim away the excess fabric. Pin and sew all seven fabric leaves onto the garment back in this manner.

**8.** Set the machine for satin-stitch applique.
**Machine Set-up:**

| | |
|---|---|
| Machine foot | Satin stitch |
| Needle | Size 80 |
| Needle thread | Embroidery, col taupe |
| Bobbin thread | Polyester |
| Feed teeth | Raised |
| Top tension | Slightly loosened |
| Bobbin tension | Normal or slightly tightened |
| Fabric | Calico |
| Stitch length | 0.5 |
| Stitch width | Vary from 1.0 to 5.0 |

Satin stitch around the raw edges and down the centre vein of each leaf on the jacket back. Keep the satin stitch widest at the stem of the leaf. Appliqué all seven leaves this way.

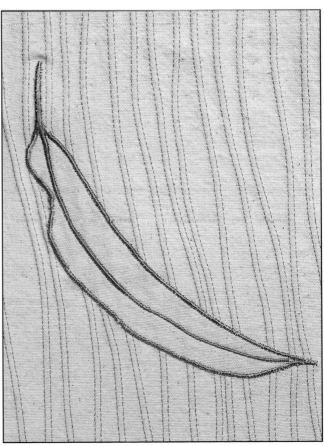

---

# TIPS
• Before marking the jacket, test the water-soluble pen on a swatch of fabric to be sure the marks will erase.
• Never iron over the marks made with a water-soluble pen; they will set indelibly.

---

**9.** Using Vliesofix, fuse two pieces of fabric wrong sides together. To do this, place one piece of fabric right side down on the ironing board, then place a piece of Vliesofix, cut

slightly smaller than the fabric, glueside down on top. Run a hot iron over the paper surface. When the glue has melted, peel away the paper. Place the second piece of fabric rightside up over the exposed glue web. Press firmly until the pieces are fused, then allow to cool.

10. Place a gumleaf on a section of the doubled and fused fabric. Position the leaf so the centre vein is on the bias grain of the fabric; this will allow the leaf to curl slightly when stitched. Draw around the leaf with a soluble marker. Trace five different leaf shapes on doubled fabric. Trace a further two leaf shapes on a single layer of biasgrain fabric these leaves will curl more freely, adding interest and variety to the work.

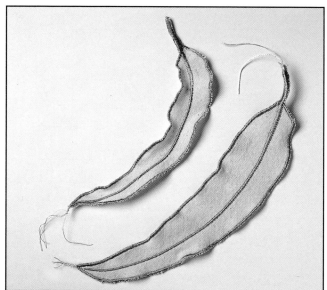

11. Set the machine for applique stitching.
**Machine Set-up:**

| | |
|---|---|
| Machine foot | Satin stitch |
| Needle | Size 80 |
| Needle thread | Embroidery, col taupe |
| Bobbin thread | Polyester |
| Feed teeth | Raised |
| Top tension | Slightly loosened |
| Bobbin tension | Normal or slightly tightened |
| Fabric | Calico |
| Stitch length | 0.5 |
| Stitch width | 1.0 to 5.0 |
| Couching cord | Crochet cotton |

Stitch around the edge of each leaf, tapering the width slightly at the tip. Stitch the centre vein over a length of crochet cotton to give a raised effect. Use small, very sharp scissors to cut out each leaf shape. Cut close to the stitching line.

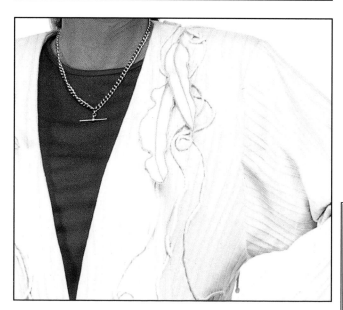

12. Satin stitch around the cut edge of the leaf, tapering the stitch width as before. This stitching must encase the initial row of satin stitch on the leaf. When nearing the leaf tip, reduce the stitch width as much as possible, then lift the foot and pull both threads away from the machine enabling a loop to be formed. Turn the leaf around and use the long thread loop to hold the leaf taut. Stitch the other side, pulling on the loop to ease the stitching over the tip. Continue satin stitching to the top of the leaf. Trim threads, adding a drop of fray-stopping liquid to prevent unravelling.

> ## TIPS
> • When cutting out gumleaves, use fray stopping liquid on any snipped stitches.
> • When using fusible products, protect the ironing board and iron soleplate from excess glue by using a teflon appliqué mat or a sheet of non stick baking paper.

13. For the twisted cord, cut several long 2.5cm wide strips of calico on the straight grain.
Set the machine for zigzag work.
Machine Set-up:

| | |
|---|---|
| Machine foot | Zigzag, bulky overlock |
| Needle | Size 80 |
| Needle thread | Embroidery, col cream |
| Bobbin thread | Polyester |
| Feed teeth | Raised |
| Top tension | Slightly loosened |
| Bobbin tension | Normal |
| Fabric | Calico |
| Stitch length | 3.0 |
| Stitch width | 1.0 to 5.0 |

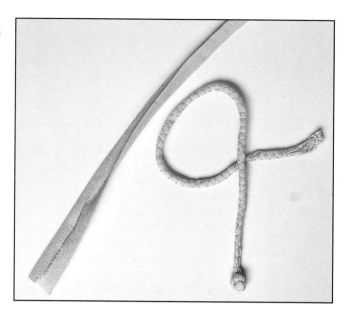

Fold long edges of the strips to centre and fold again. Place the strip under machine foot and sew a few stitches to anchor the folds at one end. Twist the fabric tightly in front of the foot and zigzag over the twisted cord. Finish with a few straight stitches. Make sure the stitching encases the cord without going through it.

14. Arrange the twisted cords on the jacket. Twist or knot where appropriate to incorporate the appliquéd leaves. Attach cords with hand stitching. Leave some areas of the cord unstitched to add more dimension.

15. The twisted cord is also used to make a loop closure and button at the front of the jacket. To make the button, knot one end of a short cord and use the length to form a coil around the knot. Place the coil onto a piece of backing fabric and straight stitch in lines radiating from the centre. Trim the backing fabric close to the stitching and treat the edges of the backing fabric with fray-stopping liquid. Attach the button with a hand-worked thread shank. Stitch a corresponding loop of cord on the opposite front. Position the loop so its raw ends will be encased in the seam allowance when the facing is applied.

16. Arrange the three dimensional leaves on the jacket, pin in place and try on the jacket to check their placement. Attach the leaves with several hand or machine stitches.

17. Complete the jacket and add lining in accordance with the pattern instructions. ✄

TIP Position the presser foot 1.5cm forward from the starting point. Select straight stitch and sew in reverse until the needle reaches the starting position. Adjust for satin stitch and sew forward covering the stitching.

# Terrific Tie-Backs

*Add a special touch to plain curtains with this embroidered curtain tie-back inspired by Australia's native flora and designed by Kristen Dibbs.*

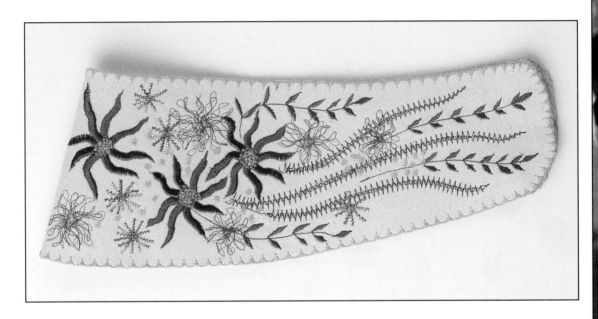

## MATERIALS

- 40cm firm calico
- 40cm heavy-weight fusible interfacing
- Polyester machine thread; soft green, yellow, beige
- Rayon machine-embroidery thread; rust, orange, variegated cream/grey/rust
- Machine feet: Open Satin Stitch or freehand embroidery
- Tracing paper and fabric-marking pen
- Two small brass curtain rings

## METHOD

1. Trace the pattern onto calico. Add 1cm seam allowances all around, then cut two pieces for front and back. Put one piece aside to be the tie-back lining.

2. Trace the pattern onto heavyweight fusible interfacing, then fuse the interfacing onto the wrong side of the calico sections.

3. Trace the embroidery design onto the right-hand side of one piece of cotton. If making a pair, reverse the design for the second piece.

4. To embroider the large rust-coloured flowers:

**Machine Set-up:**

| | |
|---|---|
| Machine foot | Open-toe Satin Stitch |
| Machine Needle | Embroidery 80 |
| Top Thread | Rayon, rust |
| Bobbin Thread | Polyester, beige |
| Top tension | Loosened |
| Bobbin Tension | Normal |
| Stitch Pattern | Zigzag |

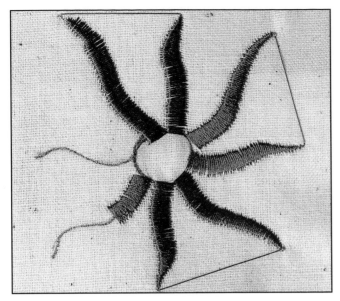

| Stitch Width | 0 to 5.0 |
| --- | --- |
| Stitch Length | 0.5 |
| Feed Teeth | Raised |

Begin at the edge of the flower centre. Bring the bobbin thread to the surface of the fabric and sew the first few stitches over the thread ends before trimming them off. Keeping the design line at the centre of the foot, sew to the end of the petal, gradually tapering the stitch width to zero and moving the fabric to create a wavy line. At the end of the petal, raise the presser foot and begin the next petal at the tip. Sew to the centre of the flower. Repeat for all petals then trim threads.

**5.** To embroider he green fern leaves:

**Machine Set-up:**

| Machine foot | Open-toe Satin Stitch |
| --- | --- |
| Machine Needle | Embroidery 80 |
| Top Thread | Polyester, soft green |
| Bobbin Thread | Polyester, beige |
| Top Tension | Loosened |
| Bobbin Tension | Normal |
| Stitch Pattern | Blind Hem |
| Stitch Width | 0 to 5.0 |
| Stitch Length | 1.5 |
| Feed Teeth | Raised |

After securing the threads, set the stitch width to 5.0 and sew to the tip of the fern leaf, gradually reducing the stitch width to zero. Sew down the other side of the fern leaf so the straight stitch forms the rib of the leaf and the zigzag stitches form the fronds. Overlap the stitch in the centre to form a rib.

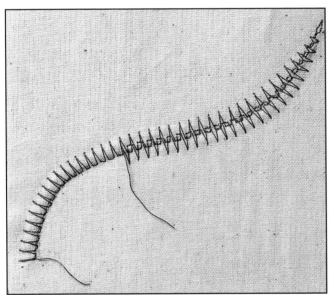

**6.** To embroider the leaves:

**Machine Set-up:**

| Machine foot | Open-toe Satin Stitch |
| --- | --- |
| Machine Needle | Embroidery 80 |
| Top Thread | Polyester, soft green |
| Bobbin Thread | Polyester, beige |
| Top Tension | Loosened |
| Bobbin Tension | Normal |
| Stitch Pattern | Zigzag |
| Stitch Width | 0 to 3.0 |
| Stitch Length | 0.5 to 2.5 |
| Feed Teeth | Raised |

Sew the leaves by tapering the stitch width from 0 to 3.0 and back to 0. Start at the tip of the first leaf and stitch towards the stem, pivot and sew the second leaf. Repeat for each pair of leaves, finishing at the tip of the top leaf. Pivot and change the stitch width to 2.5 to sew the stem.

**7.** To embroider the shaggy daisies:

**Machine Set-up:**

| Machine foot | Freehand embroidery |
| --- | --- |

| | |
|---|---|
| Machine Needle | Embroidery 80 |
| Top Thread | Polyester, yellow, rayon, orange |
| Bobbin Thread | Polyester, beige |
| Top Tension | Loosened |
| Bobbin Tension | Normal |
| Stitch Pattern | Three-step Zigzag |
| Stitch Width | 3.0 |
| Stitch Length | 0 |
| Feed Teeth | Lowered |

Begin near the centre of the daisy and, while running the machine fast, form the first petal by stitching away from and then back to the centre of the flower. Sew all petals in he same manner. Then change the thread to orange rayon and stitch a second layer of petals over the first. Finish with freehand scribble at the flower centres.

**8.** For the small multi-coloured daisies, wattles and yellow dots:
**Machine Set-up:**

| | |
|---|---|
| Machine foot | Freehand embroidery |
| Machine Needle | Embroidery 80 |
| Top Thread | Variegated rayon |
| Bobbin Thread | Polyester, beige |
| Top Tension | Loosened |
| Bobbin Tension | Normal |
| Stitch Pattern | Zigzag |
| Stitch Width | 2.0 |
| Stitch Length | 0 |
| Feed Teeth | Lowered |

Beginning near the centre of the daisies, move the fabric in a north-south direction to sew the first petal. Turn the fabric for the second petal. For the wattle and small yellow dots, sew circles of zigzag.

**9.** Embroidering the orange, machine-beaded flower centres:
**Machine Set-up:**

| | |
|---|---|
| Machine foot | Freehand embroidery |
| Machine Needle | Embroidery 00 |
| Top Thread | Rayon, orange |
| Bobbin Thread | Polyester, beige |
| Top Tension | Loosened |
| Bobbin Tension | Normal |
| Stitch Pattern | Zigzag |
| Stitch Width | 2.0 |
| Stitch Length | 0 |
| Feed Teeth | Lowered |

Begin in the centre of a large rust flower, hold the fabric still, then sew eight to ten stitches. Build into a small bead. Fill the flower centre, allowing some of the beads to flow onto the petals.

**10.** When all the embroidery is complete, trim thread ends

and press the work from the wrong side. Carefully press the seam allowances to the wrong side, over the interfacing. Clip Curves and mitre corners so the edges are smooth. Repeat for the lining piece. Pin the embroidered piece and the lining wrong sides together, checking that edges match exactly.

**11.** To embroider the edges:
**Machine Set-up:**

| | |
|---|---|
| Machine foot | Open-toe Satin Stitch |
| Machine Needle | Embroidery 80 |
| Top Thread | Polyester, beige |
| Bobbin Thread | Polyester, beige |
| Top Tension | Loosened |
| Bobbin Tension | Normal |
| Stitch Pattern | Reverse Scallop |
| Stitch Width | 5.0 |
| Stitch Length | 0.5 to 1 |
| Feed Teeth | Raised |

Beginning at the centre of one end of the tie-back, stitch around the edge of the fabric so the right-hand swing of the needle falls just over the edge of the fabric. This will join both pieces of fabric and give an attractive edge finish. Hand-sew a brass curtain ring to each end of the tie-back. ✄

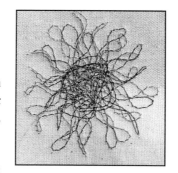 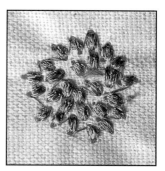

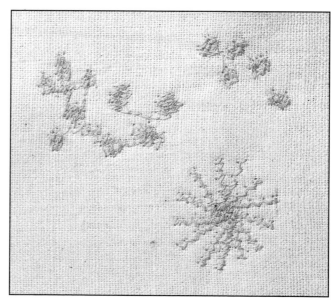

# Rural Road

*Landscape has always had a special appeal for textile artist Alvena Hall. The rolling wheat fields of South Australia's Mallee region, the red-sand deserts of the interior, the shattered rocks of the Breakaways and the quaint, dirt roads of the picturesque Adelaide Hills are all sources of inspiration for this unique artist. In this project – a cushion titled Rural Road – Alvena demonstrates how beautiful effects can be achieved by layering sheer fabrics and then quilting them together.*

## MATERIALS

- 40cm x 115cm heavy calico
- 25cm square of light wadding
- 30cm square of organza, col cream
- 25cm organza, cols light blue, light green or yellow, mid green, light grey, light tan
- Machine-embroidered threads: Madeira cols 2146 (multi-green/yellow/blue), 2004 (yellow/red/blue/pink/orange), 2006 (multi-pink/blue/grey), 2034 (multi-black/grey), 2028 (variegated green), 2025 (variegated blue), 1106 (green), 1169 (green), 1133 (blue), 1242 (blue), 1023 (yellow), 1033 (mauve), 1031 (mauve) and 1110 (grey)
- Polyester thread for the bobbin, col cream
- Machine needle: embroidery 80
- Heavy tracing paper
- Wash-out fabric marker
- 35cm dress zip, col cream

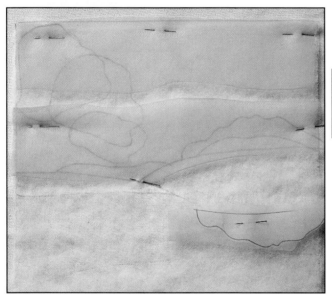

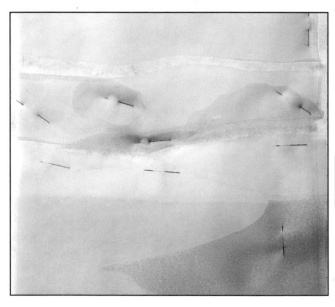

## METHOD

1. Cut calico into two pieces; 40cm x 40cm (for cushion front) and 42cm x 40cm. Tear cream organza to make a 26cm square; it is essential the organza be torn and not cut as this will stabilise the fabric and prevent fraying.

2. Trace design on page 40 onto tracing paper. Label each area of the design as shown on the pattern and use arrows to indicate the top and base of each shape.

3. Draw a 25cm square in the centre of the 40cm square of calico. Transfer the traced design onto the fabric using a washout fabric marker.

4. Pin the wadding over the calico design. Ensure the design can be seen through the wadding.

5. To make patterns for the applique fabric pieces, return to the tracing you made on paper and cut out the shapes.

6. Select a light blue sheer for the sky. When cutting out the sky in fabric, add an extra 5mm at the top and bottom edges to ensure adequate fabric for overlap. Cut the sky into two pieces along the dotted line, then spread the two pieces slightly apart to leave a white space. Position the sky over the wadding. Use light grey organza for the distant hills. Place the hills over the bottom edge of the sky.

7. Use a yellow/green organza to fill the bottom half of the design and for the distant trees. A second smaller shape of light green is placed over the first to create closer hills.

8. Cut a darker green shape and piece at the bottom right for the foreground. Use light tan organza for the road. Use shades of green for the larger rounded shapes resembling the foliage of the trees. The left-hand tree shape extends past the outline of the design.

9. When all shapes are in position, carefully place the cream organza overlay on top of the shapes and pin in position. Do not trap pins underneath. Check that everything is square and that the colours look natural. If not, make changes.

10. In all landscape embroidery, it is best to stitch the most distant features first. This means that sky and far hills will be sewn initially and fences, daisies, foliage and foreground details will be sewn last. Note how the spacing between lines of stitching varies. Avoid stitching many rows close together as this will make the embroidery appear too heavy and dark. Baste the cushion front, by machine or hand, diagonally from corner to corner and around all four sides. Check that the work is square and then set the sewing machine for free machining.

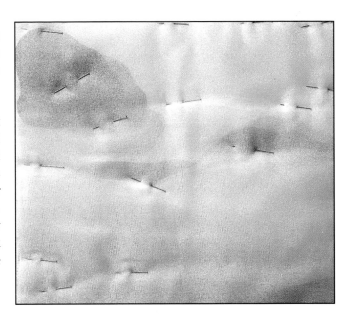

**Machine Set-up**

| | |
|---|---|
| Machine foot | Freehand embroidery |
| Needle | Embroidery 80 |
| Top thread | Embroidery, col variegated blue |
| Bobbin thread | Polyester, cream |
| Top tension | Loosened |
| Bobbin tension | Normal |
| Feed teeth | Lowered or covered |
| Fabric | Cushion top with sheer overlays |
| Stitch width | 0 |
| Stitch length | 0 |

Sew two rows of straight stitching close to the top edge to hold fabric in place. Outline the cloud shapes with a few undulating horizontal lines. Extend sewing to the edges of the calico for a casual effect.

11. Change the top thread to grey and outline the distant hills. Change thread to variegated green and stitch the hills. Stitch a few rows of yellow on the tops of the hills for a sunlit effect.

TIPS. • When working with variegated thread, one of the tones may be too dark for your work. Observe the stitching and when the dark thread approaches the needle, sew a few securing stitches and stop the machine. Loop the length of the unwanted colour out to the side, sew another one or two securing stitches and continue. Trim away the unwanted thread.
• To create subtly-coloured foliage, cut small pieces of organza in various colours and place these under the larger layers of foliage.

12. Prepare the machine for free zigzag machining in the foliage of the trees.
**Machine Set-up:**

| | |
|---|---|
| Machine foot | Freehand embroidery |
| Needle | Embroidery 80 |
| Top thread | Machine embroidery, col multigreen/yellow/blue |
| Bobbin thread | Polyester col cream |
| Top tension | Loosened |
| Bobbin tension | Normal |
| Feed teeth | Lowered or covered |
| Fabric | Cushion top with sheer overlays |
| Stitch pattern | Super stretch or variable width zigzag |
| Stitch width | 4.0 to 5.0 |
| Stitch length | 0 |

Turn the work sideways under the machine so the zigzag will create an irregular, textured effect. Do not stitch too closely. For a greener look, re-embroider some areas in green thread.

13. Use straight stitch a selection of grey threads to show the tree trunks and branches. White thread will add dimension as well.

14. Thread machine with col 2004 and revert to free straight stitch. Use irregular lines to stitch on the road. Cut away some parts of the organza overlay close to the stitching to give the road areas of stronger colour.

15. Gate posts are made from a double layer of grey organza stitched with machine embroidery thread col 2006. Use some black thread on the lefthand side of the posts to suggest a shadow. Make two fence posts and, with straight stitching, add a few strands of wire.

16. Use colours 2146, 1169 and 1106 and a varied zigzag or superstretch stitch for the grass. Cut small snips of green and blue organza and freely stitch over them for bright colour accents. Add free zigzag scribble in shades of mauve near the base of the gate posts.

17. Now add some embroidered daisies to the work.
**Machine Set-up:**

| Machine foot | Zigzag |
|---|---|
| Needle | Embroidery 80 |
| Top thread | Embroidery, yellow |
| Bobbin thread | Polyester, cream |
| Top tension | Slightly loosened |
| Bobbin tension | Normal |
| Feed teeth | Raised |
| Fabric | Cushion top with sheer overlays |
| Stitch pattern | Single daisy or freehand |

If your machine has a single pattern button, select this to sew daisies among the grass. If your machine does not have a suitable automatic flower pattern, use freehand embroidery to scribble small daisy shapes in the grass.

18. Pin the work up to eye level, move back and check the colour balance. You may need to add touches of bright yellow or blue to enliven the work.

19. Sponge design lines with cold water to remove fabric pen markings.

20. To assemble the cushion cover, cut the 42cm x 40cm piece of calico in half. Sew the zip into the centre. Undo the zip. With right sides facing, place the cushion back and front together and straight stitch all four sides. Turn through the open zip and press gently from the back. Fill the cover with the cushion insert. ✂

# Out of the Shadows

*The traditional technique of shadow appliqué and hemstitching gets a contemporary look when combined with dramatic fabric colours and an up-to-the-minute design. Sue Newtown, from ELNA has used a grey satin-backed crepe for the stunning shadow applique on an organza overskirt.*

## MATERIALS

- Silk organza, navy blue, sufficient for pattern
- Satinbacked crepe for appliqué, grey
- Tearaway fabric stabiliser
- Machine foot: zigzag
- Machine needles: universal size 70/10, wing size 100, twin 2mm ($^1/_{16}$in) and 4mm ($^1/_8$in)
- Rayon machine embroidery thread: two spools each of silver/grey and navy
- Two spools of Bobbinfil: black and white
- Handsewing needle
- Duckbill embroidery scissors
- Chalk pencil
- Spray starch

**NOTE:** Sue created her own pattern for this garment. However, any simple jacket pattern with an edge-to-edge front and without a bust dart would be suitable.

## METHOD

1. Cut out the jacket pieces in organza. Spray starch all pieces to be appliquéd.

2. Trace and cut out the large and small diamond designs onto paper. Pin the designs under the organza on the front and sleeve where the embroidery is to be sewn. The front has a small diamond at the top and two large diamonds below. The sleeve has a large diamond at the top and a small one below. Space the designs approximately 6cm ($2^3/_8$in) apart. Trace the designs using the chalk pencil.

3. Measure 2cm ($^3/_4$in) from the outside of the top diamond design and rule three parallel lines spaced 2cm ($^3/_4$in) apart.

4. Prepare for twin needle sewing.

**Machine Set-up:**

| | |
|---|---|
| Machine foot | Zigzag |
| Needle | Twin, 2mm ($^1/_{16}$in) |
| Top thread | Two spools of embroidery, silver/grey |
| Bobbin thread | Bobbinfil, white |
| Top tension | Normal |
| Bobbin tension | Normal |
| Feed teeth | Raised |
| Fabric | Organza |
| Stitch length | 2.0 |
| Stitch width | 0 |

Stitch three lines of twin needle straight stitch following the traced lines. At both ends of the stitching, pull the threads through to the back and tie them together.

5. For each diamond, cut a rectangle of grey satin-back crepe approximately 34cm ($1^1/_4$in $1^5/_8$in) larger than the shape. Cut the fabric on the straight of grain. Pin and tack the fabric diamond in place behind the drawn chalk diamond. Pin a piece of tear-away behind the grey fabric. Select a triple straight stitch pattern, length 2.0.

6. Begin sewing along the edge of the chalk lines and stitch around the traced line of the inner diamond. When completed, take the threads to the back and tie them off. Repeat for all the diamond shapes.

Carefully remove the tearaway stabiliser and replace it with a fresh piece for each round of stitching Before beginning the next step, sew a practise sample on similar fabric. Check that the stitch pattern you are using is facing the correct way. If not, use the mirror image button or sew in the opposite direction.

**7.** Select a Parisian hemstitch or a similar stitch remembering to check the stitch width. Begin to sew in a different place along the sides of the chalk line for the next row of stitching.

**8.** Sew two rows of hemstitching around each diamond. Tie off the thread ends securely at the back. Carefully remove the tearaway, using tweezers for small, stubborn pieces.

**9.** Use the duckbill scissors to trim the excess satin fabric close to the outer row of stitching.

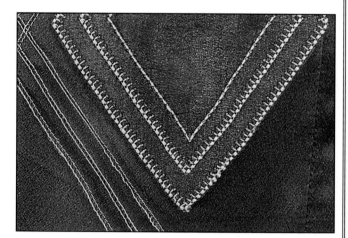

**10.** Complete the garment following the pattern instructions and finish all the hem edges with a straight stitch and a 4mm (¹/₈in) twin needle. ✂

TIP To turn the corner with a twin needle, raise the needle using the hand wheel so that the points of the needle just clear the fabric, turn the fabric and continue to sew.

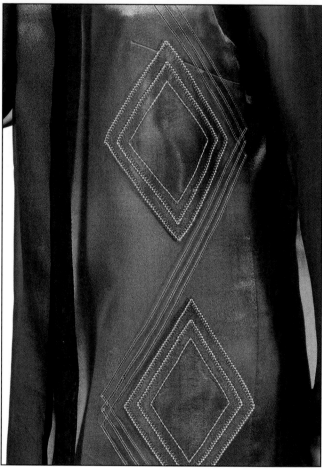

TIPS • Turning the fabric while a twin needle is down will cause the needle to break. A twin needle is wider than a regular needle so check the stitch width of all zigzag stitches and patterns by turning the hand wheel gently to see the full width of the needle swing.
• Always check that the bobbin has sufficient thread before beginning a long line of twin-needle sewing. It can be difficult to rethread inconspicuously if the bobbin thread runs out.
• Always pretest the spray starch on a scrap of fabric, especially when using darkcoloured sheer fabric.
• When pinning organza, use fine lace or bridal pins to avoid marking the fabric.

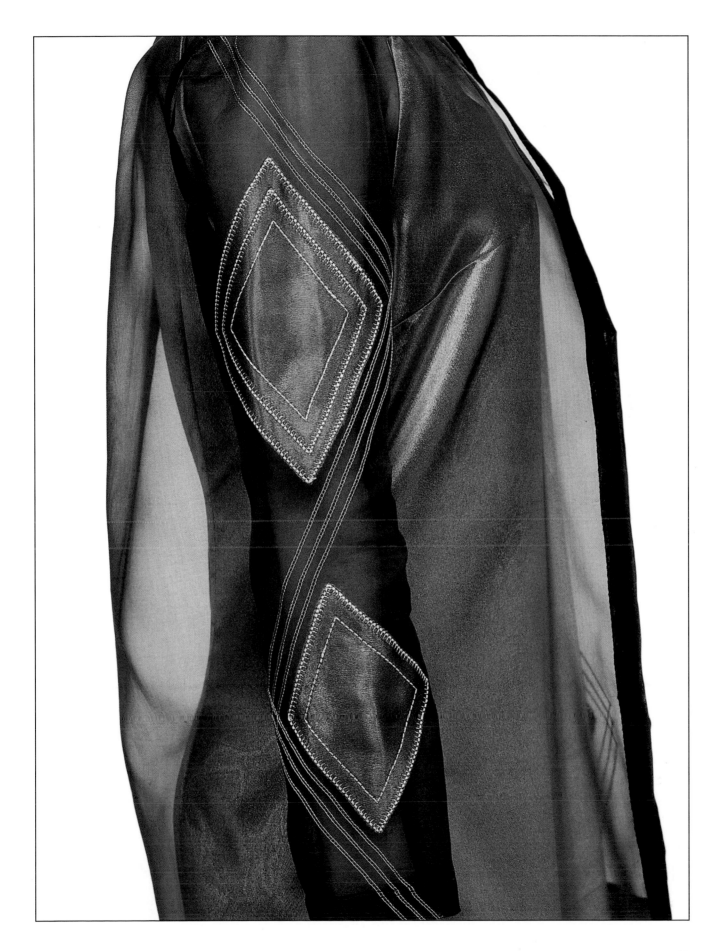

# Bargello & Seminole Quilted Jacket

*Made by Jodie Munro for Janome, this cozy jacket would be a welcomed addition to any wardrobe. Bargello and Seminole quilting techniques have been combined using stunning blue fabrics.*

## MATERIALS

- Colour 1.      60cm (24in) for bargello and seminole
- Colour 2.      35cm (15in) for bargello
- Colour 3.      35cm (15in) for bargello
- Colour 4.      2.5m to 2.9m ($2^3/_4$ to $3^1/_4$yd) for bargello, mid section, seminole
- Colour 5.      35cm (15in) for bargello
- Colour 6.      35cm (15in) for bargello
- Colour 7.      60cm (24in) for bargello and seminole
- Colour 8.      3.9 to 4.2m ($4^3/_8$ to $4^5/_8$yd) for bargello, lining and piping
- Jacket pattern of your choice without a collar
- 1.2 to 1.5m ($1^3/_8$ to 2yd) cotton wadding
- 3.4m muslin (3 ° to $4^3/_8$yd) for interlining
- 8 covered buttons
- $^1/_4$in diameter cotton piping cord
- Thread to match
- Presser feet, piping, satin stitch, zipper, Walking and 6mm(1/4in) patchwork foot
- Rotary cutter, cutting board and ruler
- Machine needles, Universal size 12/80 and Janome blue tip
- Quilters fabric marking pencil
- Embroidery thread to match or compliment mid-section fabric design
- Optional: shoulder pads

NOTE: Pre-wash and iron all fabrics, wadding and muslin.

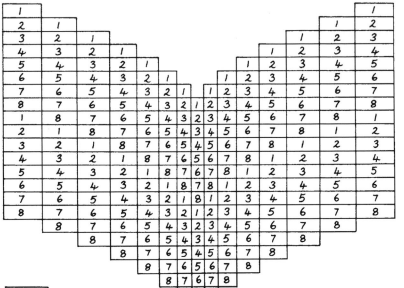

Diagram 1
Back

Diagram 2
Front Right

## METHOD

### Pattern Preparation

1. Trace the front, back and sleeve pattern pieces adjusting the length as required.

2. Do not include the hem allowance and facings when tracing as the edges will be piped and the jacket will be lined.

3. Cut the front pattern fabric at the fold line, eliminating the facing.

4. Cut the back pattern fabric piece with the seam line on the fold of the fabric.

## BARGELLO PATCHWORK

### Jacket Back

1. Cut two $1^1/_2$in strips of each of the eight fabrics.

2. With the right sides of the fabrics together, join the strips using a $^1/_4$in foot.

3. Press all the seams in one direction.

4. From the joined fabrics, cut a 1in strip then cut two strips each of $1^1/_4$in, $1^1/_2$in, $1^3/_4$in, 2in, $2^1/_4$in, $2^1/_2$in, $2^3/_4$in and 3in.

5. Piece the strips together offsetting the fabric colours by one square. See diagram1.

### Jacket Front

1. Cut two $1^1/_2$in strips from each of the eight fabrics.

2. With the right sides of the fabrics together join the strips using a $^1/_4$in foot.

3. Press the seams in one direction.

4. From the joined fabrics, cut two strips each of $1^1/_4$in, $1^1/_2$in, $1^3/_4$in, 2in, $2^1/_4$in, $2^1/_2$in, $2^3/_4$in and 3in.

5. Piece the strips together offsetting the fabric colours by one square as before. See diagrams 2, 3 and photograph A.

Photograph A

## Jacket Sleeves

1. Cut four 1¹/₂in strips of each of the fabric colours No I to7 and cut six strips of colour No 8.

2. With the right sides of the fabrics together join the strips using a ¹/₄in foot.

3. Press the seams in one direction.

4. Cut two 1in strips and cut four strips each of 1¹/₄in, 1¹/₂in, 1³/₄in, 2in, 2¹/₄in, 2¹/₂in, 2³/₄in and 3in.

5. Piece the strips together offsetting the fabric colours by one square as before. See diagram 4.

## SEMINOLE PATCHWORK

### Jacket and Sleeve Hems

1 Cut six 1¹/₂in strips of colour No1 (A), cut six 1¹/₄in strips of colour No 4 (B) and cut three 1¹/₄in strips of colour No 7 (C).

2. Using the ¹/₄in foot and with the right sides of the fabrics together, join the strips following the order shown in diagram 5. Press the seams in the same direction.

3. Cut the joined fabric into 1¹/₄in strips

4. Piece the strips together offsetting the fabric colours by one square as before. See diagram 6. Press the seams in one direction

5. Sew the piping along one edge of the joined fabrics. See diagram 7 and photograph B.

Diagram 3
Front Left

Diagram 4
Sleeve

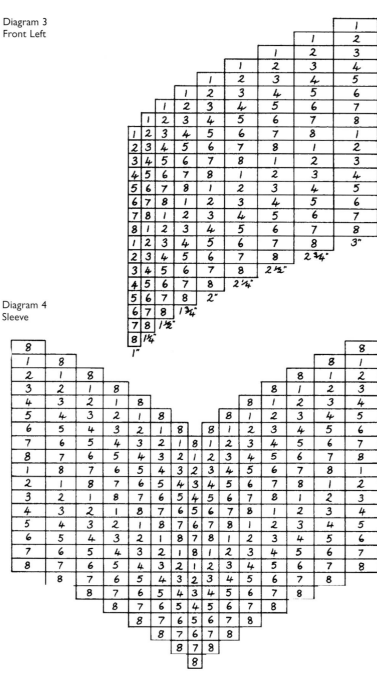

Diagram 5

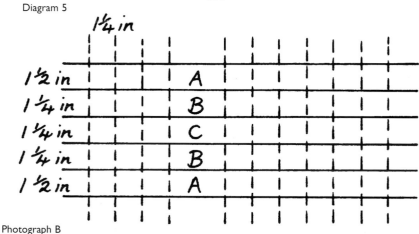

Photograph B

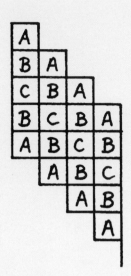

Diagram 6

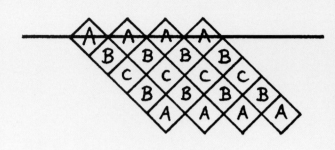

Diagram 7

## TO COVER PIPING CORD

1. Cut the piping cord to the length required and cut a 1¼in fabric strip to the same length as the cord.

2. Attach the piping foot to your machine and select the centre needle position.

3. Cover the cord with the fabric and place it in position in the left or right groove of the presser foot.

4. Stitch as close as possible to the side of the cord. See diagram 8.

## TO ATTACH THE PIPING

1. With the raw edge of the piping level with the raw edge of the fabric place the piping on the right side of the fabric.

2. Lower the left groove of the piping foot over the piping cord.

3. Sew the piping cord to the edge of the fabric, guiding the cord into the groove of the foot as you stitch. See diagram 9.

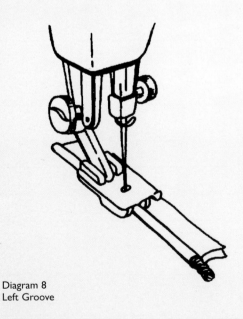

Diagram 8
Left Groove

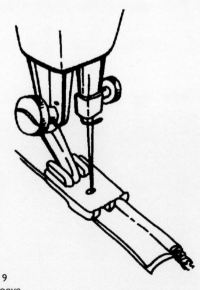

Diagram 9
Right Groove

## OVERLOCKER BUTTON LOOPS

**NOTE:** This is a great way to make button loops that wont fray and as an extra bonus they are easy to turn.

1. Cut a narrow length of fabric to make the button loops.

2. Prepare the overlocker for a close three-thread stitch and sew a length of chain 5cm (2in) longer than the fabric strip.

3. Lay the chain on the right side of the fabric strip. See diagram 10.

4. Fold the fabric over the chain ensuring the chain is laying close to the folded edge.

5. Place the raw edges of the strip under the presser foot of the overlocker and stitch along the edge trimming the excess fabric. See diagram 11.

6. Pull the chain slowly until the fabric begins to roll, continue pulling the chain to turn the fabric to the right side. See diagram 12.

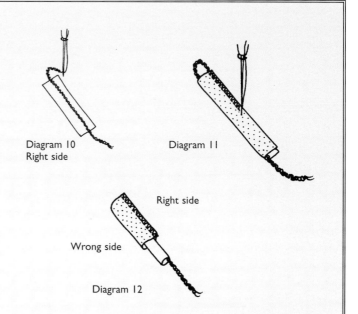

Diagram 10
Right side

Diagram 11

Right side

Wrong side

Diagram 12

**NOTE:** Make sure the chain remains close to the folded edge of the fabric so it will not be cut by the overlocker blade or enclosed in the seam. The chain must remain free so it can be used to pull the fabric through to the right side. The same technique can be used on the sewing machine.

## JACKET CONSTRUCTION

1. Determine the finished length of the jacket and sleeves. Attach the mid fabric sections of the jacket to the bargello pieced fabric inserting the piping between the fabrics as shown. See diagram 13 and photograph C.

2. Attach the seminole strip to the lower hem edge of the front, back and sleeve pieces.

3. Pin the wadding and muslin to the back of the fabric pieces and quilt them as shown in diagrams 14, 15 and 16.

4. Using a quilters marking pencil, trace all the pattern pieces onto the quilted fabrics. Make sure that the shoulder seams and sleeve heads are matching.

5. Baste over the traced lines and cut the pieces out.

Photograph C

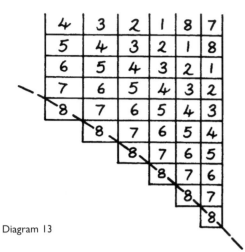

Diagram 13

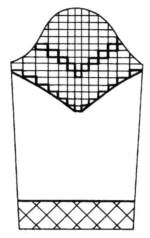

Diagram 14.
Sleeve

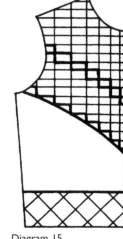

Diagram 15
Front

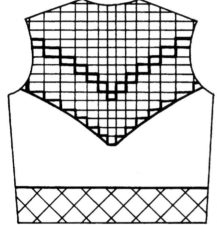

Diagram 16
Back

6. Using the walking foot, sew the shoulder seams, darts (if any) and side seams together.

7. Using the satin stitch foot and embroidery thread, define selected pattern areas on the mid section fabric with a narrow satin stitch.

NOTE: Jodie selected some of the leaves to highlight on the fabric shown here. Triple straight stitch has been used to sew along the centre leaf vein.

8. With the right sides of the fabric together, join the side seams of the sleeves. Ease the sleeve heads and pin, baste and then stitch the sleeves into the jacket.

9. Make the button loops as described in diagrams 10 to 12 and baste them in position on the front of the jacket.

10. Attach shoulder pads if desired and sew the piping cord to the outside edges of the jacket. Pin, baste and stitch the lining in place and finish by attaching the buttons to the front of the jacket. ✄

# Technique Tutor

## THE CIRCULAR-SEWING ATTACHMENT

Despite its unusual appearance, a circular-sewing attachment is remarkably easy to use. You can create many delightful designs simply by varying the machine stitch, needle and thread type. Here's how it works.

The style of the circular-sewing attachment and the way it is attached to the machine will vary according to the individual machine make and model. The way it works and the result it produces, however, are very similar.

The attachment has an adjustable pin that can be positioned at certain distances from the centre needle position on the throat plate of the machine. The fabric is either placed securely in an embroidery hoop or stabilised very well to keep it firm. This not only allows for decorative embroidery or satin stitches to be sewn without the fabric puckering but also assists in keeping the fabric an equal distance from the needle.

The fabric is pressed down over the pin to hold it at an equal distance from the satin-stitch or embroidery presser foot. The fabric can turn easily on the pin creating a pivot point in the centre of the fabric. When sewing is commenced the raised feed dogs pull the fabric forward, the fabric turns in a complete circle as it pivots on the pin, requiring only a minimum of guidance.

A variety of different-sized circles can be stitched at an equal distance apart by moving the pin closer to or further away from the needle.

## TIPS FOR FREE-MOTION SEWING
### THE CORRECT FOOT

Q Which foot is recommended for free-motion embroidery. Why can't a regular foot be used?

A Specialised freehand embroidery feet are available for certain machines. While some feet have open toes and others are made from clear plastic, both features are aimed at giving optimum visibility. If these are not available the darning foot is a common alternative. Unlike other presser feet, these specialised feet do not touch the machine throat plate and consequently have no effect on the movement of the fabric placed

Darning foot

Open-toe embroidery foot

underneath. This allows the fabric to be moved and manipulated freely in any direction.

Q Why use a foot at all if it doesn't touch the fabric?

A When free-motion sewing with the darning foot, the needle pierces the fabric without any support on either side of the penetration point. The fabric can cling to the needle and is easily pulled upward with the needle each time it is raised. The darning foot assists in keeping the fabric down, close to the throat plate of the machine, and the bottom of the foot pushes the fabric away from the needle as it rises. Some darning feet are spring loaded to do an even better job.

## LOWERING THE FEED DOGS

Q Why must the feed dogs be lowered?

A When free-motion stitching, it is important to lower the feed dogs of the machine. By lowering the feed dogs, the fabric can be moved freely in any direction as it is not gripped by the teeth of the feed dogs. When the feed dogs are in motion they work in conjunction with the presser foot to feed the fabric smoothly and evenly in a straight line towards the back of the machine. We require the fabric to be moved in many different directions not just a straight line.

## STITCH-LENGTH DIAL

Q If the fabric is moved manually under the needle, why must the stitch length be reduced?

A Even though the stitch length is being controlled manually, the movement of the feed dogs is still being controlled by the stitch-length dial. The longer the stitch length the larger the movement of the feed dogs. When the feed dogs are lowered they sit underneath the throat plate of the machine. If the stitch-length dial is not turned to 0, the feed dogs will still move as the machine is sewing. Over time, this continual movement will cause unnecessary wear on the machine parts.

## LOWERING THE FOOT

Q Why must the presser foot be lowered?

A It is easy to forget to lower the presser foot when free-motion stitching. The foot is always in a higher than normal position and may look like it has already been lowered. Remember to double check for this every time before stitching as lowering the foot engages the thread tension disc. By simply raising and lowering the presser foot, thread locks and tangles can be avoided.

# Time for Tea

*This delicate embroidered scone holder created by Elsie Jaensch for Husqvarna will add a touch of old-fashioned elegance to your next afternoon tea party. Dust off Grandmother's precious bone china tea cups, polish up the family silver and enjoy tea, petits fours and of course, hot scones.*

## MATERIALS

Machine embroidery threads:
- DMC 30, col 3325, light blue
- DMC 50, col 3325, light blue
- Isacord, col 2171. pink
- Isacord, col 0453 green
- DMC 50, col white for construction

**Other:**
- 3 x 35cm squares of cotton of linen fabric col white
- 4.75m cotton edging approx. 20mm wide
- lm x 3mm wide ribbon
- Machine feet: opentoe embroidery and zigzag
- 50cm square of thick cardboard, for lace shaping
- Machine needles: embroidery 80 and wing needle
- Spray starch
- Fabric-marking pen
- Tear-away stabiliser
- Machine embroidery hoop

These instructions were designed for a Husqvarna Orchidea Machine. The embroidery pattern used is No 71106841 Diamond Collection from the Husqvarna embroidery library. If you do not have this machine , follow the instructions and substitute similar machine or hand-embroidery patterns.

1. Cut 3 x 35cm squares of fabric. Trace the scone holder patter onto each piece of fabric, ensuring that the pattern is centred in each square.

2. Trace the design and candlewick stitching lines onto one square of fabric. On the other squares, trace only the candlewick stitching lines. These should be placed onto the teardrop sections of the shape.

3. Place Husqvarna embroidery template on the first square of fabric. mark centre point and placement lines. This will make it easier when positioning the fabric into the hoop.

4. Select design No 71106841 from Husqvarna embroidery library and prepare the machine for embroidery. The design will use DMC 30 col 3325 and Isacord cols 2171 and 0453. Place tear-away stabiliser behind fabric and put both into embroidery hoop, matching placement lines and centre point. Embroider alternate sections on the scone-holder shape.

**For other machines:**
**Machine Set-up**

| | |
|---|---|
| Machine foot | Automatic pattern |
| Needle | Embroidery 80 |
| Needle thread | Rayon or cotton embroidery threads in selected colours |
| Bobbin thread | Embroidery, in matching colours |
| Top tension | Loosened |
| Bobbin tension | Normal |
| Feed teeth | Raised |
| Fabric | White fabric stretched in hoop |
| Stitch length | Automatic |
| Stitch width | Automatic |

Embroider an automatic motif or group of pattern stitches in three alternate sections of sconeholder shape.

**5. Candlewick stitching**
**For Husqvarna machines:**
Program the following sequence into an empty machine memory:

| | |
|---|---|
| Zigzag stitch A 12 | Length 0, width 2 x 9 times |
| Straight stitch A2 | Length 1.5 x 2 times |
| Straight stitch A2 | Length 1 x 1 times |

Use DMC 30. col 3325 in needle and bobbin. Using an open-

toed foot and with tearaway placed behind the fabric, sew candlewick stitch on marked stitch lines on all three squares of fabric.

**For other machines:**

**Machine Set-up**

| | |
|---|---|
| Machine foot | Automatic pattern |
| Needle | Embroidery 80 |
| Needle thread | Embroidery in selected colours |
| Bobbin thread | Polyester in toning colours |
| Top tension | Loosened |
| Bobbin tension | Normal |
| Feed teeth | Raised |
| Fabric | Stretched in hoop |
| Stitch length | Automatic |
| Stitch width | Automatic |

Stitch rows of decorative patterns along lines marked for candlewick stitching, re-positioning the fabric in hoop as required.

### 6. Lace shaping

Place the right side of fabric square onto cardboard. Shape and pin lace around pattern edge by placing straight edge of lace onto outside edge of marked pattern line. Pull top heading thread of lace to gather edge, so it will lie flat around curves. Spray starch lace, press carefully and remove from the board.

### 7. Attaching Lace

**Machine Set-up**

| | |
|---|---|
| Machine foot | Zigzag or open-toe |
| Needle | Embroidery 80 |
| Needle thread | Embroidery |
| Bobbin thread | Embroidery |
| Top tension | Normal |
| Bobbin tension | Normal |
| Feed teeth | Raised |
| Fabric | White cotton |
| Stitch pattern | Zigzag or Husqvarna stitch A12 |
| Stitch length | 1 |
| Stitch width | 1 |

Sew the inside edge of the lace onto the fabric on all the three squares.

### 8. Trimming fabric

Trim fabric edge to width of 1cm from stitching. Clip curves and press towards back of fabric. Straight stitch on right side of fabric 2mm inside first stitching. Trim excess fabric next to straight stitching. Repeat for each square. You will now have three embroidered and lace edged circles.

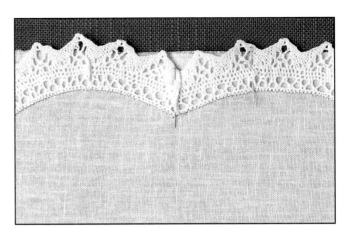

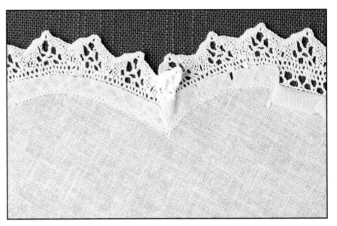

**Machine Set-up**

| | |
|---|---|
| Machine foot | Zigzag, or opentoe |
| Needle | Wing |
| Needle thread | Embroidery |
| Bobbin thread | Embroidery |
| Top tension | Normal |
| Bobbin tension | Normal |
| Feed teeth | Raised |
| Fabric | White cotton with tear-away stabiliser |
| Stitch pattern | Triple zigzag or Husqvarna D6 |
| Stitch length | 2.5 |
| Stitch width | 2 |

Sew wing needle zigzag along inside edge of lace on all three circles of fabric. This will create a pattern that is decorative on both front and back.

9. Place fabric circles one and two right sides together. Using previous setting or Husqvarna hemstitch D75, stitch together along placement lines.

10. Position circle three underneath joined circles. Fold curved edges of top layer back. Sew 2nd and 3rd layers together in centre of each section. Begin sewing from outside edge of section at centre of curves. Stitch towards centre of scone holder.

11. Attach lengths of ribbon to scone holder at marked positions. Tie ribbons together to form shape of the scone holder. ✂

# TrellisTreasure

*A longline vest is wonderfully flattering and versatile. Here, GAI HAVILAND, from Elna, shows how you can add a distinctive touch, with trellis bars, appliquéd and three dimensional leaves, and trailing vines made from beautiful novelty yarn.*

## MATERIALS

- Longline vest pattern
- Raw silk for vest, plus an extra 50cm (²/₃yd)
- Whisperweft interfacing, sufficient for vest
- Lining, for vest
- Three 50cm (²/₃yd) lengths of toning fabric for trellis bars
- Two 30cm (12in) lengths of contrasting fabric for applique
- One reel of polyester thread in toning colour
- Five reels of rayon machine embroidery thread to tone with contrast fabric
- One reel of metallic machine embroidery thread, silver
- 1 reel of fine cord or crochet cotton to edge leaves
- Machine needle: embroidery 80
- Machine needle: universal 80
- Machine feet: zigzag, satin stitch or open toe embroidery, couching foot
- 1m (1yd) Vliesofix paper backed fusible web
- 50cm (²/₃yd) tear away fabric stabiliser (optional)
- 1 ball Panda Renoir acrylic yarn or novelty yarn in toning colour
- Light fading marking pen

## PREPARATION

Prewash Whisperweft according to manufacturers instructions, and dry flat. Do not iron.

and from hem to hip on left front. The stitch pattern used on Gai's vest is a combination of one small circular unit followed by two straight stitches. Select a suitable automatic pattern stitch and sew a few test samples on scrap fabric to determine your chosen pattern.

> **TIP** If the fabric puckers during embroidery, use a tearaway stabiliser underneath the material.

4. Appliquéd leaf shapes: Make a paper pattern for appliqué by drawing around a real leaf, approximately 5cm–8cm (2in–3in) long, and 3cm (1³/₁₆in) wide. Fuse a piece of Vliesofix to each piece of contrasting fabric, trace and cut out five leaves from each contrast fabric. Arrange the leaves over the previously embroidered areas and when you're satisfied with the placement, remove the paper backing from each leaf and fuse to the garment fabric.

> **TIP** Tearaway stabiliser underneath fabric ensure smooth stitching during applique.

5. Prepare the machine for appliqué.
**Machine Set-up:**

| | |
|---|---|
| Machine foot | Embroidery |
| Machine needle | Embroidery |
| Needle thread | Embroidery, to match fabric |
| Bobbin thread | Polyester, to match fabric |
| Feed teeth | Raised |
| Top tension | Loosened |
| Bobbin tension | Normal |
| Fabric | Raw silk with appliqué |
| Stitch pattern | Zigzag |
| Stitch | 0.3–0.5 |
| Stitch width | 0–4.0 |

Begin at the base of each leaf with stitch width 2.0, gradually increasing stitch width to 4.0 at the widest part of the leaf and tapering to 0 at the point. Sew the centre vein, from tip to base, tapering width from 0.5 to 2.0. Repeat for each leaf, then remove the stabiliser from behind the embroidered area.

6. Trellis bars: Prepare machine for straight stitching.
**Machine Set-up:**

| | |
|---|---|
| Machine foot | Zigzag |
| Machine needle | Universal 80 |
| Needle thread | Polyester to match fabric |
| Bobbin thread | Polyester |
| Feed teeth | Raised |
| Top tension | Normal |
| Bobbin tension | Normal |

## METHOD

1. Cut out vest pattern pieces in raw silk, lining and interfacing. Fuse interfacing to wrong side of raw silk.

2. For the trellis bars, from each length of toning fabric cut four strips each 7cm (2³/₄in) wide, across full width of fabric. From the raw silk, cut bias strips 6cm (2³/₈in) wide to be used for binding edges of vest.

3. Prepare the sewing machine for embroidery.
**Machine Set-up:**

| | |
|---|---|
| Machine foot | Satin stitch/embroidery |
| Machine needle | Embroidery 80 |
| Needle thread | Metallic silver |
| Bobbin thread | Polyester, colour to match fabric |
| Feed teeth | Raised |
| Top tension | Loosened |
| Bobbin tension | Normal |
| Fabric | Raw silk, fused to interfacing |
| Stitch pattern | Automatic |
| Stitch length | Automatic |
| Stitch width | Automatic |

Sew three rows of your chosen automatic pattern as follows: From shoulder to hip of right front and right back

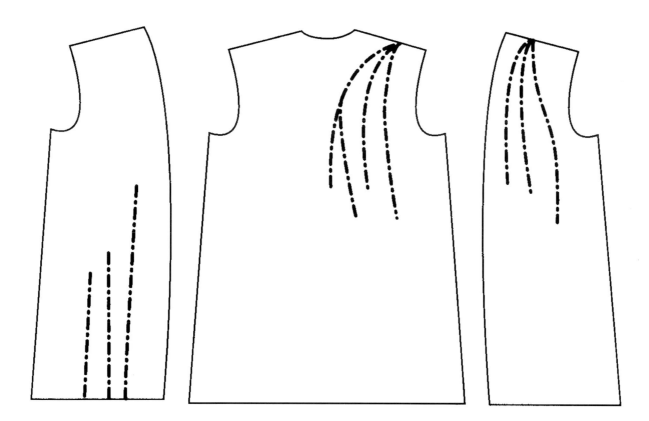

| | |
|---|---|
| Fabric | Strips of raw silk |
| Stitch pattern | Straight |
| Stitch length | 2.5 |
| Stitch width | 0 |

Fold fabric strips in half lengthwise with right sides and raw edges together. Stitch a 6mm (¹/₄in) seam down each strip, then turn the strips right side out and press with seam under centre of each strip.

**7.** Position the strips 5cm (2in) apart over the appliquéd areas at the shoulders and lower front. Ensure one raw end of each strip extends into a seam allowance at the garment edges. Weave the strips over and under each other and pin them in place. Turn in all raw ends of strips which end on the body of the garment and press. Using a straight or a decorative pattern stitch, sew down the centre of each strip, catching the folded raw ends.

**8. Three dimensional leaves:** Fuse Vliesofix to remaining contrast fabric, remove paper backing, fold fabric in half and fuse to produce a double sided fabric. Trace about 25 leaves onto the double sided contrast fabric and cut them out 1cm outside of the traced lines.

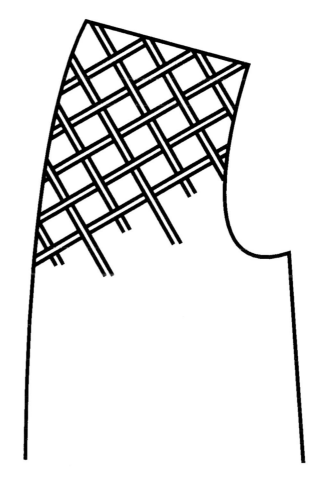

9. Prepare machine for edge stitching.

**Machine Set-up:**

| | |
|---|---|
| Machine foot | Embroidery |
| Machine needle | Embroidery 80 |
| Needle thread | Embroidery, to match fabric |
| Bobbin thread | Embroidery, to match fabric |
| Feed teeth | Raised |
| Top tension | Loosened 23 degrees |
| Bobbin tension | Normal |
| Fabric | Double sided contrast fabric |
| Stitch pattern | Zigzag |
| Stitch length | 1.0 |
| Stitch width | 0.8 |

Stitch a narrow line of zigzag over the traced line on each leaf. Remove the leaf from the machine leaving 15cm (6in) thread tails which will be used as handles to help move the leaf under the needle when edge stitching. Use small sharp scissors to trim away excess fabric close to stitching. Change stitch width to 2.5 and stitch length to 0.3 0.5.

10. Place the cut edge of the leaf under the centre of the foot. Thread fine cord through the hole of the couching foot or place a length of fine cord under the heel and over the toe of the foot. Use your left hand to hold the end of the cord and the 15cm (6in) tails of thread firmly together behind the machine foot. Lower the presser foot, and use your right hand to hold and guide the cord in front of the foot. Stitch around the edge of the leaf, with the needle entering the fabric on the left hand swing, and going just outside the fabric on the right hand swing. Gently pull the thread ends with the left hand to help the fabric feed smoothly under the needle. Stop with the needle in the fabric when you reach the point of the leaf.

11. Make a loop of cord around the first finger of your right hand, then bring the cord to the front. Sew halfway down the side of the leaf using the loop of cord as a handle. Stop and gently pull the end of the cord, so the loop disappears into the stitching and continue stitching to the end of the leaf. Arrange the leaves over the trellis and pin to check placement. Attach each leaf by stitching a vein down the centre, as in step 5.

12. Arrange the fancy yarn in gently curving lines over the trellis and the leaves and pin. Prepare machine for couching.

**Machine Set-up:**

| | |
|---|---|
| Machine foot | Embroidery |
| Machine needle | Embroidery |
| Needle thread | Embroidery to tone with wool |
| Bobbin thread | Polyester to match garment |
| Feed teeth | Raised |
| Top tension | Loosened |
| Bobbin tension | Normal |
| Stitch pattern | Zigzag |
| Stitch length | 2.0 |
| Stitch width | 1.5 |

Couch carefully over the wool.

13. **Garment construction:** Join the shoulder seams of the vest and the lining. Join the side seams. Pin the garment and the lining together around the armholes and the entire outside edge with a 1.5cm ($^5/_8$in) seam allowance. Stitch together using a toning polyester thread. Cut away excess fabric outside stitching.

14. Press bias strips in half lengthwise, open out and press raw edges to the centre fold. Fold in half lengthwise again and press. Open out folded bias strip and with right sides together, pin the strip to the armhole, matching raw edges. Cut ends of strip on the diagonal and sew a narrow seam to form a circle which matches the length of the armhole. Fingerpress the seam open, then stitch the binding to the armhole, following line of crease pressed into bias strip.

15. Fold the bias strip to the wrong side of the armhole, then pin and hand or machine stitch in place. Join further bias strips to make sufficient length to bind entire outside of the vest in the same way. ✂

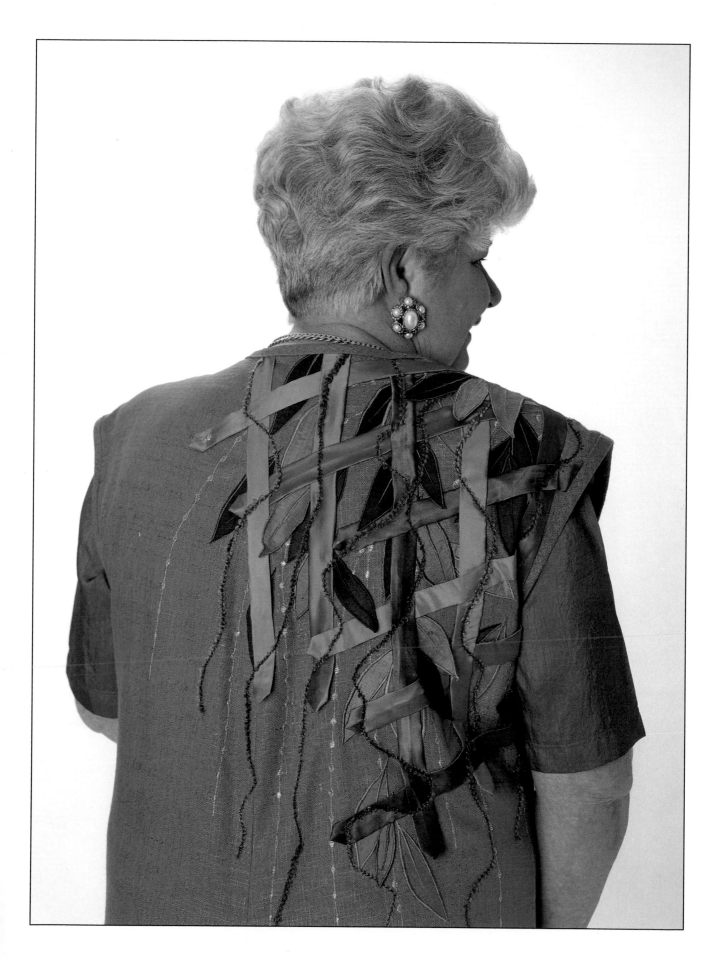

# Baby, Look at You

*Hey baby, you'll get all the glances in this Nordic style bonnet and booties. Designed and made by Corrie Diespstraten, these infant essentials were created in soft felt for babyís comfort and embellished with faux buttons, decorative machine stitches and tiny French knots. The pieces are designed for a six month-old baby.*

## MATERIALS

- 40cm x 95cm (½yd x 1yd) felt, white
- 40cm (½yd) flannelette, white, for lining
- Machine feet, zigzag, buttonhole, satin stitch, darning
- Machine needles, embroidery size 80/12, twin needle size 2.5mm
- Machine embroidery threads, medium blue and dark blue
- Metallic thread, gold
- Bobbinfil
- Two skeins DMC stranded embroidery cotton, white
- Three skeins DMC stranded embroidery cotton, dark blue
- Hand sewing needle
- Water-soluble fabric marking pen

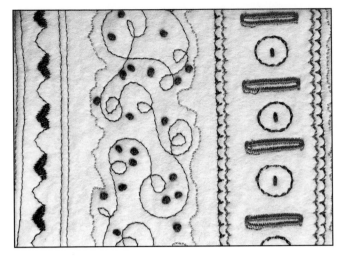

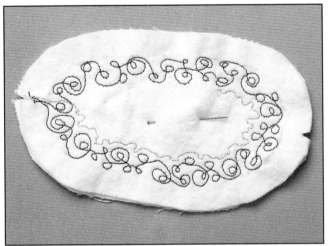

## MEHTOD

1. On a piece of paper, trace the patterns for bonnet and booties. For the bonnet back, draw a circle with a 12.5cm diameter (4$^7/_8$in). Add the embroidery details and 1cm ($^3/_8$in) around all the pieces for the seam allowances. Cut out paper patterns.

2. Pin the patterns to the felt and cut out the pieces.

3. Draw the embroidery design onto the felt with a fabric marking pen.

4. On the sewing machine, insert the twin needle and attach the satin stitch foot. Wind the bobbin with Bobbinfil. Thread the dark blue embroidery thread from the right-hand spool pin, to the right side of the tension disc, then through the right-hand needle. Thread the medium blue thread from the left-hand spool pin, to the left side of the tension disc, then through the left needle. Slightly loosen the top tension.

5. Select a decorative stitch pattern. Ensure the pattern and stitch width can be safely used with a twin needle. Gently turn the hand wheel to test one full stitch. If the stitch width is too wide, reduce it as required. You may also use your twin needle regulating button, if you have one.

> TIP Never turn the fabric while the twin needle is down. The needle will twist and break.

6. Follow the pattern for the sequence of stitching on the bonnet front, back and booties. Sew the first row of stitching, following the line marked on the fabric. Sew the second row in the opposite direction, using the edge of the first row of stitching, as a guide for the edge of the machine foot. Sew lines one, two and three in patterned stitches and lines four and five in straight stitch.

7. Insert the size 80/12 machine needle and attach the buttonhole foot. Use the dark blue thread to sew a row of 1cm-long ($^3/_8$in) buttonholes on the bonnet front and four buttonholes on the bonnet back. As the buttonholes are decorative, they should not be cut open.

8. Attach the darning foot, either lower or cover the feed dogs. Set the stitch length and width to zero and slightly loosen the top tension. Use the dark blue embroidery thread to sew small freehand circles, to simulate buttons, between the buttonholes and freehand swirls and scribbles in the areas shown on the pattern.

9. Sew a row of pattern stitches between the two rows of twin needle straight stitch.

10. Use the gold metallic thread to sew a wandering freehand line on both sides of the blue swirls and between the rows of twin needle pattern stitch.

> TIP Practise on scrap fabric before sewing on your work.

11. Thread a hand needle with six strands of blue cotton. Sew French knots on the bonnet and bootie pieces arranging the knots among the blue thread scribble.

12. Remove the markings from the fabric with a damp sponge. When the marks are erased, use a warm iron to press the fabric on the wrong side.

13. Make a twisted cord for tying the bonnet and booties. For the bonnet, cut two one-metre (1¹/₈yd) lengths of blue and white stranded embroidery cotton. This will make one cord. For the booties, cut two 80cm (⁷/₈yd) lengths to produce one cord. Make two cords for the bonnet and four cords for the booties.

## MAKING TWISTED CORD

To make the twisted cord on the sewing machine, thread the stranded cotton through the holes of an empty bobbin. Place the bobbin on the bobbin winder on top of the machine. Engage the bobbin winding mechanism, hold the ends of the cord firmly above the machine and run the machine at a medium speed allowing the machine to twist the cord.
When the cord begins to twist back on itself, stop the machine. Keep tension on the cord and fold it in half. Take the cord from the bobbin. Hold the cut ends together and release the folded end allowing the cord to twist together freely. Firmly knot the ends to prevent unravelling and trim the ends to form a tiny tassel. If your machine does not have a top winding bobbin, make the twisted cord by hand. To do so, tie both ends of stranded cotton together to form a circle. Slip one end of the circle over an empty spool pin on your machine and slip a pencil into the other end to twist the cord. When well twisted, fold the strands in half and knot.

## CONSTRUCTION

### Bonnet

1. Cut the bonnet back, front and booties form flannelette. Thread the machine needle and bobbin with white thread. Prepare the machine for straight stitching, raise the feed dogs, set the tension to normal and attach the zigzag foot. Sew the centre back seam on the bonnet fronts. Press the seam allowances open.

2. Pin and sew the bonnet back in place on both the flannelette and felt sections.

3. Pin the bonnet and lining with the right sides together. Pin the cord in position at the front corners. Sew the sections together, leaving a small opening at the back edge.

4. Turn the bonnet to the right side and then sew the opening closed with small hand stitches. Press the edge.

### Booties

1. Cut the booties in lining.

2. Pin the tops and lining with the right sides together, pin the ties in place and stitch the top edges. Trim the edge and clip the seam allowance at the corners.

3. Turn right side out, Pin the centre back seams with the right sides together. Sew the centre back seam in a continuous motion through the felt and the lining. Trim the seam and turn to the right side. Press.

4. Pin the sole lining to the wrong side of the sole. See photograph 2. Then pin to the wrong side of the upper bootie, matching the markings for the centre front and back. Sew the seam and finish the edge.

5. Turn the bootie right side out and make a small buttonhole or eyelet for the ties. ✂

# PATTERN AND STITCH DETAIL

## For Bootees and Bonnet

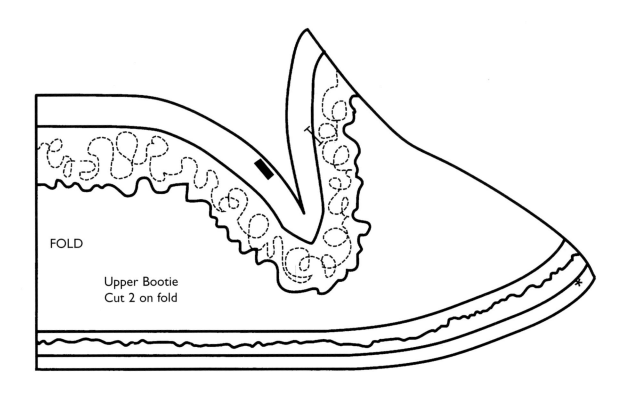

FOLD

Upper Bootie
Cut 2 on fold

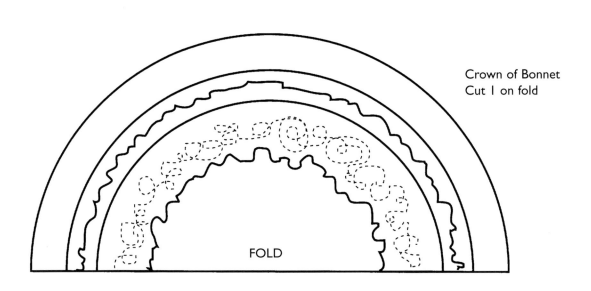

Crown of Bonnet
Cut 1 on fold

FOLD

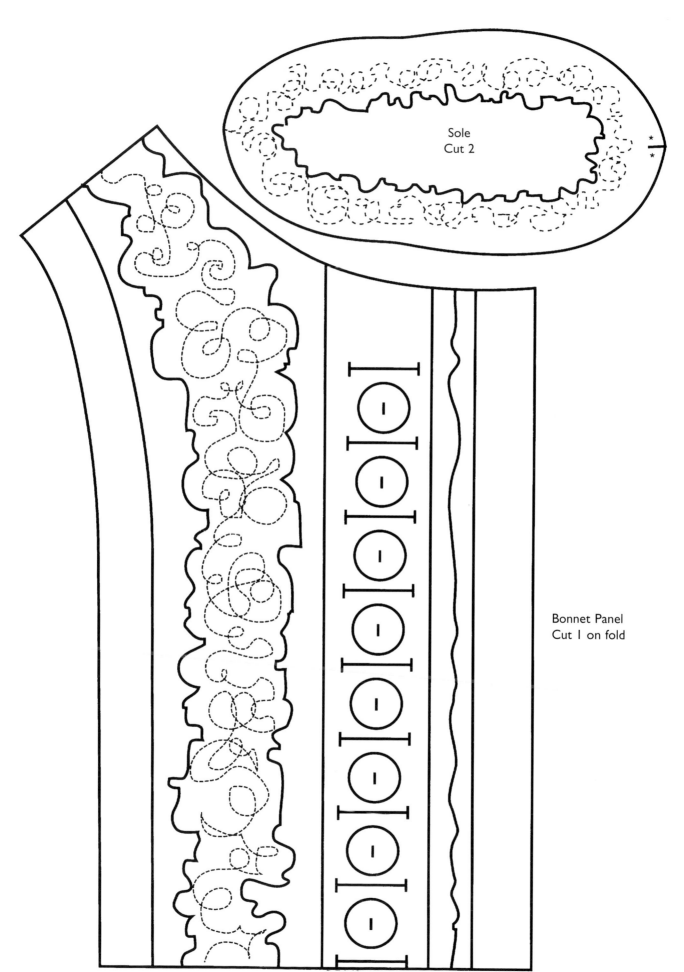

Sole
Cut 2

Bonnet Panel
Cut 1 on fold

# Hats off to Summer

*Whether you're off for day at the beach or travelling to an exotic overseas location, this collapsible sunhat by LORRAINE GILL makes the perfect partner. Fold it flat for easy storage, then pop it up and slip it onto your head for picture-perfect sun protection. Petersham-ribbon-covered wires create a piped effect to offset a range of feminine embroideries created on Husqvarna's Orchidea and Rose machines.*

## MATERIALS

- 50cm (20in) 20/20 millinery canvas
- 5m (5$\frac{1}{2}$yd) cotton-covered millinery wire
- 1m (40in) cotton chambray fabric, blue
- 50cm (20in) cotton-interlock fabric, white
- 4m x 25mm (4$\frac{1}{2}$yd x 1in) petersham ribbon, navy
- 2m x 15mm (2$\frac{1}{3}$yd x $\frac{5}{8}$in) petersham ribbon, navy
- Felt-and-straw stiffening liquid
- Rayon machine-embroidery threads
- Polyester thread for assembly
- Clear fabric glue

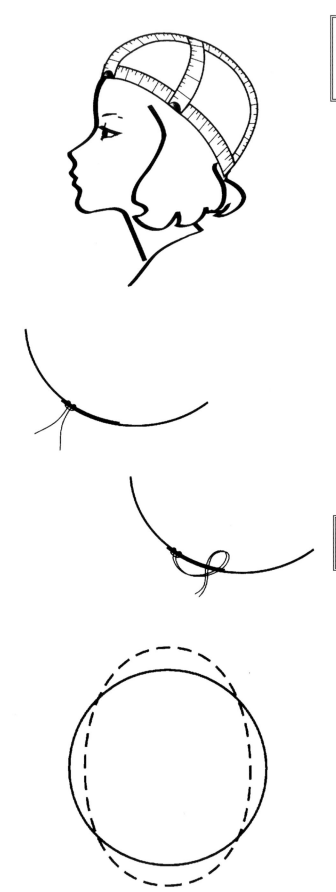

TIP It is important to use millinery-quality viscose and cotton petersham ribbon as it can be moulded smoothly around the brim.

1. Determining your head size: The head-fitting measurement is taken firmly around the forehead and over the occipital prominence, or bump, at the base of the head. Measure around your head to determine the length of wire needed for the hat. The crown size is determined by measuring from the forehead, at the hairline, to the nape of the neck and then measuring from the tip of one ear to the other.

2. Preparing the wire: The head wire should be about 1cm (³/₈in) larger than your head measurement plus 7cm (2³/₄in) for joining. Example: If your head measurement is 57cm (22¹/₂in), the wire should measure 58cm (22⁷/₈in) plus 7cm (2³/₄in) to give a total length of 65cm (25⁵/₈in). Shorter lengths of wire are cut for the crown rings, so the circles of decreasing size will fit inside each other when the hat is folded flat. Each ring is overlapped 7cm (2³/₄in) when joined. Cut six lengths of wire as follows:
- For the inner brim, cut two wires to match your head size plus 7cm (2³/₄in)
- For the top crown ring, cut one 53cm
- For the third crown ring, cut one 55cm
- For the second crown ring, cut one 59cm
- For the first crown ring, cut one 61cm

TIP When cutting wire, pull it from the inside of the coil and cut with wire cutters.

3. To make the headwires: Form each length of wire into a circle, overlapping the ends by 6cm (2³/₈in). Secure the wire with closely worked hand-buttonhole stitch. To do this, cut a 1m (40in) length of thread and fold it in half. Using your fingers, loop the fold over the wire, pull the ends through the loop and make tight. Continue until the join and the ends of the wire are completely covered.

4. Head shapes are oval, not round. To achieve the perfect oval, draw a circle to match the head wire, then measure 6mm (¹/₄in) in for each side and 6mm out from top and bottom. Connect markings to form the oval. In doing this, you will retain the correct headsize but create a more realistic shape for your head. Push the headwire circle gently but firmly and without bending, until it follows the shape of the oval. The join should be placed at centre back.

5. Forming the brim: The oval you have drawn is the starting point for the brim. Place the wire oval on the bias

grain of the canvas as shown. Trace around the wire then measure 10cm (4in) out from the oval, all around to create the brim shape. Measure 15mm (5/8in) in from the head wire line to mark the seam allowance. Cut out the brim and the middle section which will forms one layer of the crown.

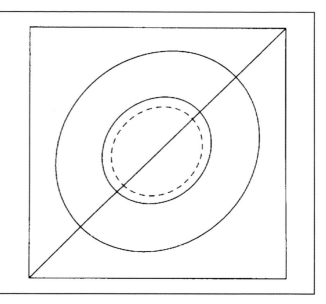

6. Place the inner-brim head wire oval on the head size line drawn on the brim. Ensure the join is at centre back, then, using a medium-width zigzag stitch on the machine or working by hand, stitch in place. If sewing by machine, ensure the needle does not hit the wire. Zigzag stitch the remaining length of wire to the edge of the brim centering the join at about 10cm (4in). Cut off any excess wire. Snip the inner edge of the brim canvas to the wire at 2cm (³/₄in) intervals and fold the seam allowance up.

7. Cut a strip of canvas 15mm x 60cm (⁵/₈in x 24in). Using zigzag stitch, sew the strip to the remaining inner-brim headwire. Place this over the turned seam allowance, overlap the ends and back-stitch by hand to form a headband on the brim.

8. **Preparing the crown:** Place the shortest length of cut wire at the edge of the canvas crown and sew the wire to the canvas using zigzag stitch. Place the crown shape onto a piece of canvas and trace around it. Mark a 15mm (⁵/₈in) seam allowance all round and cut out. Place the smaller oval on top and zigzag over wire again. The double layer will increase the strength of the crown.

9. The canvas must be stiffened to hold its shape during wear. Paint the straw-and-felt stiffening liquid onto the upper and lower sides of the canvas brim and top section of the crown.

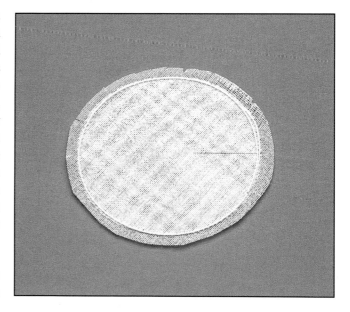

10. Covering the under brim: When the stiffener is dry, place the canvas brim onto the chambray fabric, match grainlines and cut a fabric brim 2cm (³/₄in) larger all round than the canvas brim. Place the underside of the canvas brim on the wrong side of the fabric piece. Pin the two layers together around the outside edge of the brim, stretching the fabric taut as you go. Do not pull too tightly or the brim will buckle. Straight-stitch just inside the brim wire. Trim off excess fabric. Tack firmly just inside the headwire at the inner edge of the band. Cut the crown section from the centre of the taught brim, leaving a 1.5cm (⁵/₈in) seam allowance. Snip the seam allowance of the fabric close to the headwire so it can be turned up neatly and tacked to the underside of the band.

11. Place the cotton interlock over the upper side of the brim and cut out the centre oval. Lightly glue the interlock

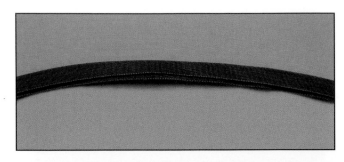

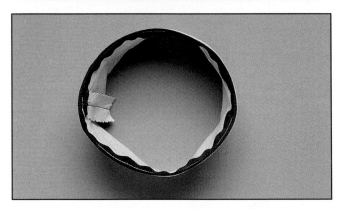

to the inner edge of the brim, then glue it to the outer edge, stretching it slightly as you go.

12. Place the brim onto chambray, ensuring the centre front is aligned with the bias grain of the fabric. Cut the chambray slightly larger than the brim. Draw the inner and outer brim outlines onto the chambray with a light-fading fabric-marking pen. Place the crown top onto the chambray, aligning the centre of the crown with the straight grain of the fabric. Draw the outline the of crown top, then reduce by 1.5cm (⁵/₈in). To allow for hooping during embroidery, cut a square of chambray which is larger than the crown top.

13. The hat pictured was embroidered using Husqvarna Embroidery card No 17. Patterns 3, 11 and 25 were placed around the brim and in the centre of the crown top. However, you may choose to decorate the brim with an automatic embroidery, or leave it plain.

14. When the embroidery is complete, cut out the centre section of the brim leaving a 1.5cm seam allowance. Snip the seam allowance to the inner-brim stitching line. Place the embroidered fabric over the canvas band and back-stitch by hand at the junction of the band and the brim. Stretch the fabric so it is taut, as you did with the underside, and pin it to the outer edge. Machine-sew against the inside edge of the outer wire. The fabric should lie smooth and flat.

15. Edging the brim with petersham ribbon: Cut the 25mm-wide petersham ribbon slightly longer than the length required to fit snugly around the edge of the brim. For easier application, fold the ribbon lengthwise so one side is slightly higher than the other. Steam-press and gently stretch the ribbon to form a curve that will follow the shape of the brim edge. Place the ribbon over the edge of the brim to determine the exact length required. Remove and join ends with a narrow seam. Trim the seam allowance ends at an angle to reduce bulk. Slide the ribbon onto the brim edge and sew with a stitch length of about 2.0.

16. Crown top and sides: Cover the prepared canvas crown top with the embroidered fabric. Stretch the fabric so it is taut and pin firmly. Stitch by machine as close to the wire on the seam allowance edge as possible. Line the crown by gluing the fabric to the underside. This will be caught at the seam allowance when attaching the sides.

17. Cut six 9cm x 65cm (3⁹/₁₆in x 25⁵/₈in) bias strips in chambray. Seam three of the strips into circles, each to fit a finished crown wire. Repeat with the other strips, they will form the lining.

18. Cut lengths of 25mm (1in)-wide petersham ribbon to fit around each of the remaining wire circles. Join each length of ribbon with a narrow seam and press the seams open. Fold the ribbons in half lengthwise over the wires and stitch by machine as close to each wire as possible to form wired pipings.

19. Sew a bias chambray band to the 48cm (19in) petersham-covered wire.

20. NOTE: When constructing the crown, ensure all joins are placed at the centre back. Stitch a chambray bias circle to the edge of the underside of the crown top. Sew as close to the wire as possible using a piping or zipper foot.

21. Slide the 48cm (19in) wire with attached bias strip onto the top of the crown to frame the edge with a navy piping. Allow all seam allowances to fall in the same direction and sew through all thicknesses of the seam allowance.

22. Pull the bias strips down and measure 3cm (1³/₁₆in) from the petersham-covered wire and position the next-size wire at

that marking. Stretch the bias strip to fit the larger wire and sew as close to the wire as possible. Trim seam allowances.

23. Add another bias strip to the inside and the outside of the second crown-ring wire and sew as close to the wire as possible. This will line the crown while it is being constructed. Repeat for the third crown-ring wire. Stitch around the last bias strip just below the 3cm (1³/₁₆in). marking and trim.

24. Attaching crown to brim: Fold 25mm-wide petersham ribbon over the brim band. Stretch and pin the last bias strip to the band, back-stitch by hand and glue the seam allowance to the inner edge of the band, making sure it will not show when the hat is worn.

25. Attach the 15mm-wide petersham ribbon to the inside band to form a head band.

26. To make the decorative bow for the hat, fold and sew 15mm (⁵/₈in)-wide petersham into flat loops and then form these into a flat bow. ✄

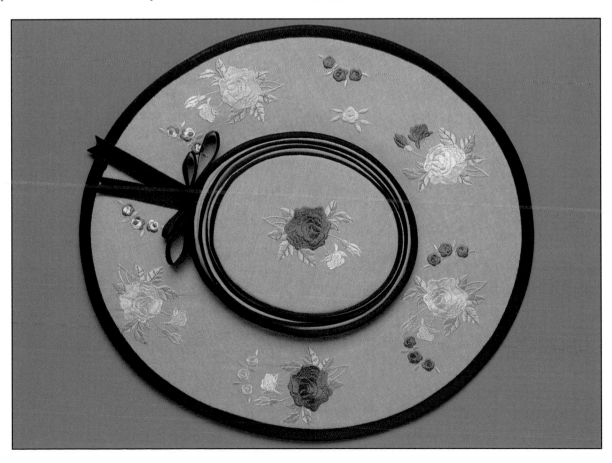

PHOTOGRAPHY: TIM CONNOLLY • STYLING: ROBYN WILSON

# Machine Embroidery Glossary

**APPLIQUE MAT:** A Tefloncoated sheet used to prevent hot irons sticking to fusible fabrics.

**AUTOMATIC PATTERN STITCHES:** Repeating decorative stitch patterns set into the machine. May be sewn according to inbuilt settings or adjusted manually for width and length.

**BACKING FABRIC:** Fabric on which the embroidery or applique is sewn.

**BOBBIN WORK:** An embroidery technique used for decorative effects such as Whip Stitch and Cable Stitch. The thicker threads used in this technique require altered bobbin tension.

**CABLE STITCH:** Embroidery technique where a thicker thread is used with a loose tension on the bobbin and a standard thread is used with normal to slightly increased top tension. Embroidery is worked on the wrong side of the fabric, so the decorative thick thread will show on the right side.

**CORNELLI WORK:** A decorative stitch pattern which moves in meandering, rounded lines which do not intersect or touch. Often used with bobbin work to give an attractive, corded effect.

**COUCHING:** The technique of stitching heavy yarns, cords and threads to the surface of fabric.

**COUCHING FOOT:** Sewing machine foot made with one or more grooves or holes to hold cord in position while being stitched.

**FREEHAND EMBROIDERY FOOT:** Machine foot suitable for freehand machine embroidery when the feed teeth are disengaged, lowered or covered. The foot allows the fabric to be freely moved while stitching. Also known as a darning foot.

**MACHINE EMBROIDERY HOOP:** Two circles of wood, cane metal or plastic, which fit together tightly to allow fabric to be stretched and held firm during embroidery. The smaller the hoop, the more tightly the fabric can be stretched.

**METALFIL NEEDLE:** A type of machine needle specially designed for fine, silky and metallic machine embroidery threads. A large Tefloncoated reinforced eye keeps friction to a minimum and prevents threads from shredding.

**OPEN-TOE FOOT:** Machine foot with a wide groove underneath and an open front to provide improved visibility of the needle entering the fabric. Also useful for couching flat braid or ribbon.

**PAINT MARKER:** A marking pen filled with white, oilbased paint. Available in sizes fine medium and bold. Useful for marking water erasable fabric where a waterbased pen is not suitable.

**SATIN STITCH:** Wide, close zigzag stitches used to form a silky, ribbonlike effect. Used chiefly in applique.

**SATIN STITCH FOOT:** Machine foot with wide groove underneath to allow easy passage over raised areas of satin or pattern stitching.

**SERPENTINE STITCH/THREESTEP ZIGZAG:** A utility stitch where the needle sews running stitches in a zigzag pattern. Serpentine stitch has a wavy appearance. Threestep zigzag has a more angular appearance.

**SPRING NEEDLE:** Used in machine embroidery, this needle is fitted with a spring and is used without a freehand embroidery foot.

**STABILISER:** Fabrics or liquid stiffening which support base fabric during embroidery. When work is complete, the stabiliser is removed by tearing away or dissolving in water.

**TWIN/TRIPLE NEEDLE:** Two or three machine needles attached to single shank. Used for decorative effects on fabric where the two or three top threads and a single bobbin thread pull up fabric into a small pintuck. Also available with embroidery needles for using with embroidery threads.

**WALKING FOOT/DUAL FEED FOOT:** A machine foot which incorporates a feedteeth mechanism to assist the even feed of fabric while stitching. Useful for pile fabrics, slippery fabrics and quilting.

**WHIP STITCH:** Freehand embroidery technique using fine thread in the bobbin with very loose tension and standard top thread and normal to tight top tension. Run the machine very fast and move the work very slowly, so the bobbin thread is drawn up to whip round the top thread, giving the appearance of fine cording.

**UTILITY STITCHES:** Basic stitches used for garment construction. Many of these can also be used decoratively.

**ZIGZAG FOOT:** Machine foot with slotted, flat base to promote correct formation of zigzag stitches.

# Index

*Machine Embroidery projects
are in italics*

Aisenberg, Rachel 23
Appliqué 6, 13, 17, 26, 60, 77
appliqué mat 17, 48, 94
automatic pattern stitches 94
*Baby, Look at You 82-87*
backing fabric 94
*Bargello & Seminole
Quilted Jacket 68-70*
bargello patchwork 66
Begg, Bonnie 44
Benson, Dorothy 23
*Black Swans 10-15*
blanket stitch 7
bobbin work 94
bobbin fil thread 7, 28
bonnet 82
bonnet pattern 86-87
booties 82
bootie pattern 86-87
braiding foot 4
bulky overlock foot 47
cable stitch 94
candlewicking foot 4
candlewick stitch 4
changing bobbin tension 37
changing top tension 37
chemical stabilisers 37
circular-sewing attachment 71
Cornelli work 94
couching 94
couching foot 94
*Country Cottage Cushion 38-43*
cushion 4, 16, 38, 54
Dacron batting 14, 17
Darning foot 30
Dibbs, Kristen 50
Diespstraten, Corrie 82
dressmakers square 18
duckbill embroidery scissors 60, 62
Elna 60, 77
embroidery hoops 37
Embroiderers' Guild of NSW 83
*Enchanted Ghost Gums 44-49*
enlarging a design 12

fabric coil button 47
fabric painting 30, 36
feed dogs 71
fray stopper liquid 46
free-form appliqué 46
freehand embroidery foot 94
free-motion sewing 71
gathering foot 8
Gill, Lorraine 88
Hall, Alvena 54
hat 88
*Hats off to Summer 88-93*
Haviland, Gai 77
*Hearts & Flowers 4-9*
*heart templates 17*
heirloom ladder stitch 4,9
Husqvarna 4, 72, 88
interfacing 4, 30
jacket 24, 44, 64
Jaensch, Elsie
Janome 64
Jenkins, Larraine 4
Lawtie, Margaret 24
*Little Blue Wren 30-36*
Long line vest 77
*Machine Embroidery from the Past 23*
machine embroidery hoop 24, 72, 94
*Machine Embroidery Tips 37*
marking pens 6
Merrett, Stewart 10
metalfil needle 94
millinery canvas 88
monofilament thread 4, 6
Munro, Jodie 64
Newtown, Sue 60
open-toe foot 94
*Orient Express 24-29*
*Out of the Shadows 60-63*
overlocker button loops 69
overlocker tweezers 7
overshirt 60
paint marker 94
Pfaff 24
piping 22
Price, Colleen 30
quilting guide 66
ribbon floss 7

*Rural Road 54-59*
ruffler attachment 8
satin stitch 94
satin stitch foot 94
seminole 64, 67
securing thread ends 37
serpentine stitch/three step zigzag 94
shadow effect, velvet 13
silk dupion 4, 24
silk ribbon 4
silk ribbon leaves 7, 9
silk ribbon roses 7, 9
solvy 30, 34
spray adhesive 12
spring embroidery hoop 4
spring needle 94
stabiliser 94
stitch-length dial 71
*Start Shading 71*
tailors' chalk 18
tear-away stabilisers 24, 37, 60, 72, 76, 77, 78
*Terrific Tie Backs 50-53*
*The Happy Heart Cushion 16-22*
three-dimensional embroidery 28
three-dimensional appliqué 44, 77
*Time for Tea 72-76*
Tips 6, 17, 13, 14, 24, 26, 27, 28, 32, 33, 34, 36, 37, 42, 46, 47, 48, 56, 57, 62, 78, 84, 85, 90, 93
treadle machine 23
*Trellis Treasure 77-81*
triple straight stitch 4
Townsend, Marilyn 38
twin/triple needle 62, 84, 94
twisted cord 47, 85
using a hoop 37
utility stitches 94
variegated threads 40, 42, 57
variegated silk ribbon 7
Verstraeten, Gabriella 16
Vliesofix 4, 17, 62
walking foot/dual feed foot 94
water soluble pen 47, 82
whip stitch 94
zigzag foot 94

Published by
Craftworld Books
A division of Express Publications Pty Ltd, ACN 057 807 904
Under licence from EP Investments Pty Ltd, ACN 003 109 055 (1995)

2 Stanley Street
Silverwater NSW 2128
Australia

First published by Craftworld Books 1999

Copyright ( Text and illustrations: Express Publications Pty Ltd 1999
Copyright ( Published edition: Craftworld Books 1999

Editor  Coleen Price
Designer  Claudia Balderrama

Photographers  Tim Connolly, Daniel Jones, Patrick Jones, Andrew Payne, Bob Peters, Tim Robinson, David Wallace
Stylists  Lynn Cook, Kristen Dibbs, Abbie Mitchell, Peach Panfili, Robyn Wilson

National Library of Australia Cataloguing-in-Publication data

The Magic of Machine Embroidery

Includes index
ISBN 1 875625-05-4

1. Machine Embroidery

Printed by KHL Printing Co, Singapore

Australian distribution to supermarkets and newsagents by Network Distribution Company, 54 Park Street, Sydney NSW 2000 Ph (02) 9282 8777.

Overseas Distribution Enquiries  Godfrey Vella  Ph 61 (2) 9748 0599, Locked Bag 111, Silverwater NSW 1811 Australia
Email: gvella@expresspublications.com.au